The **Essential** Buyer's Guide

ALFA ROMEO

ALFASUD

All saloon models from 1971 to 1983 and
Sprint models from 1976 to 1989

Your marque expert:
Colin Metcalfe

T0386222

VELOCE PUBLISHING

THE PUBLISHER OF FINE AUTOMOTIVE BOOKS

www.veloce.co.uk

First published in May 2017 by Veloce Publishing Limited, Veloce House, Parkway Farm Business Park, Middle Farm Way, Poundbury, Dorchester, Dorset, DT1 3AR, England.
Fax 01305 250479/e-mail info@veloce.co.uk/web www.veloce.co.uk or www.velocebooks.com.

ISBN: 978-1-845840-07-5 UPC: 6-36847-04007-9

Readers with ideas for automotive books, or books on other transport or related hobby subjects, are invited to write to the editorial director of Veloce Publishing at the above address.
British Library Cataloguing in Publication Data – A catalogue record for this book is available from the British Library.
Typesetting, design and page make-up all by Veloce Publishing Ltd on Apple Mac. Printed in India by Imprint Digital (UK).

Introduction
– the purpose of this book

Introduction

The Alfasud was produced by a design team gathered by Alfa Romeo under the Austrian engineer Rudolf Hruska. The project was to design an entirely new, small family car from scratch, and to build it in a completely new factory, to be sited in the under-developed region close to Naples in the south of Italy: hence the name Alfasud – sud being Italian for south.

Hruska started his career with Porsche and VW, so it was not surprising that he opted for a flat-four boxer engine, though, in this case, it was mounted in the front, and had a conventional water radiator rather than air cooling. This engine layout allowed a low bonnet line for good visibility, a low centre of gravity, and a compact – yet surprisingly spacious – body designed by Giorgetto Giugiaro of Ital Design fame. It was coupled to a longitudinally-mounted, in-line gearbox and differential driving the front wheels.

Despite its small engine, the Alfasud impressed from the start with its superb handling, roadholding, and high cruising speed, enhanced by all-disc brakes, a good driving position, a swift, light gearchange, and exceptional quietness and refinement. Its packaging was a revelation – the short engine allowing it to be a surprisingly capacious small car – the only disadvantage being pedals heavily offset towards the centre of the car in order to clear the front wheelarch.

Looking at the Alfasud now, it's hard to believe it wasn't a hatchback from the start, but this layout was unusual in 1971 when the car was launched, tending to be confined to more utilitarian vehicles such as Citroën's 2CV. The Alfasud's hatch came ten years later, giving the car a new lease of life into the mid-1980s.

Another clever derivative came first: the three-door, Giugiaro-designed Alfasud Sprint of 1976; Alfa Romeo wisely exploiting the 'sud's great handling and performance by creating from it a stylish sports coupé that would endure five years beyond its parent.

The all-new Alfasud arrives!

Rust-proofing was improved in 1977 and 1978, but the cars still suffered due to the use of extremely poor quality base steel: only Series IIIs from 1980 offered just-acceptable rust resistance. While later cars have the best specifications, early survivors are equally appealing for their rarity – and some models were scarce even when new. Just 5899 Giardinetta estates (not sold in the UK) were built, the rarest being the 1350cc version. Mechanical parts supply is reasonable, as much was carried over to the 33, and even the 145/146, although, with the disappearance of these, some 'sud parts are becoming harder to source.

The refined flat-four boxer engine.

The UK has an active enthusiast base with dedicated suppliers, so Alfasud ownership – if you keep the rust at bay – can be very rewarding.

Thanks

The author would like to thank Euan Colbron of CP Garage Services, Alan and Mandy Porter at Advantage VBRS Limited, Peter Grummitt of Alfasud Parts Online, John Christopher of JustSuds, Stephen Parry of Mr Sud fame, and Louise West for their kind assistance in putting together this guide.

The enthusiast's view!

Contents

The Essential Buyer's Guide™ currency
At the time of publication a BG unit of currency "●" equals approximately £1.00/US$1.26/Euro 1.18/$AUD1.67. Please adjust to suit current exchange rates using Sterling as the base currency.

1 Is it the right car for you?
– marriage guidance

Tall and short drivers
The driving position of an Alfasud – in common with similar Italian cars from the period – typically means that drivers with longer arms and shorter legs are more likely to be the most comfortably accommodated!

The steering wheel can be adjusted for height, however, and drivers of all statures may benefit from the simple mechanical modification of unbolting the front seats and swapping the spacers. If you use the thicker rear spacers under the front of the seat runners, and the thinner front ones under the rear (swap the bolts as well), you'll raise the leading edge of the seat base, making it far more comfortable, and giving you far more support under your knees.

Weight of controls
The Alfasud's non-assisted steering is light and direct on the move but is relatively heavy at slow speeds, while its all-round disc brake setup will stop the car without drama, as long as the system is well maintained.

Will it fit your garage?
With dimensions of 4.02m (13ft 2in) maximum length and 1.59m (5ft 3in) width, a 'sud or Sprint will fit comfortably into a standard 5.00m (16ft 6in) x 3.00m (9ft 10in) single garage; the 3.00m width allowing the driver's door to almost fully open.

Interior space
Despite its compact dimensions, spaciousness is one of the areas where the 'sud excels, with its tall cabin and relatively long wheelbase maximising interior space. For a car of such compact dimensions, the Alfasud makes excellent use of what space there is. In fact, four people can be seated in the car with adequate amounts of head and legroom all round.

Luggage space
All 'suds and Sprints feature respectable luggage compartments, with the Sprint in particular having a bigger boot than many other larger family cars of the period. Later Alfasuds gained a hatchback, which improves accessibility and practicality.

Running costs
Depending on engine size, you should expect around 25 to 37mpg (8.8 to 10.6kpl) from your Alfasud or Sprint.

Usability
All Alfasuds can cope with modern traffic conditions. Motorway cruising is perfectly possible, even in early

Even the Sprint, although quite low to the ground, allows easy access.

four-speed cars, although later five-speed models – with their better spread of gear ratios – are more relaxing and less noisy at speed. All-round visibility is good, thanks to slim body pillars and large glass areas.

Parts availability
Nearly all mechanical and service parts are available from a good network of specialists. Body parts tend to be expensive, with some – particularly for the Sprint – in very limited supply.

Insurance
Alfasuds and Sprints are not often these days given a group rating but, instead, can be insured on a Classic Car Policy. Agreeing to a limited annual mileage can often reduce premiums, while owners clubs can usually offer competitively priced, everyday cover through accredited insurers.

Investment potential
Prices for 'suds and Sprints have been on the up in recent times. Well-kept and regularly maintained examples will, at the very least, hold their values, with some rising in value considerably.

Foibles
Alfasuds and Sprints all suffer to some degree from fragile electrics (more often than not caused by poor earths), with the earliest cars being the worst for this. Pay particular attention to the column control stalks. Unusually, these two stalks control not only the indicators, lights, horn, windscreen wipers and washers, but also the two-speed heater fan as well!

Apart from very late Sprint models, which inherited the later Alfa Romeo 33's more conventional front disc/rear drum braking system, even the most basic 'suds have disc brakes all round: the fronts mounted inboard and the handbrake operating on the front wheels. The rear brake callipers can become sticky in operation, or even seize due to the efficiency of the oversize front brakes making the rears semi-redundant, due to their intrinsic under-utilisation in normal operation.

The rear boot (trunk) lid – or hatchback on later models – can only be opened from inside the car by means of cable operation, via a lever beside the front seats.

Plus points
Find a fine Alfasud of any model and you'll be rewarded with an exceptionally pleasurable and satisfying car to drive. It handles brilliantly, and really enjoys being thrown into the bends. The sound of the flat-four boxer engine at full chat is infectious and, due to the 'sud's superb refinement, you could use your car as everyday transport should you wish.

Minus points
Early cars had virtually no rust-proofing, which led to severe corrosion. Beware, too, of previous poor bodywork repairs or restoration as rampant rust may well return.

Alternatives
Citroën GS, Ford Fiesta, Honda Accord, Renault 5, Chrysler Sunbeam, Fiat 128 3P, VW Scirocco, Lancia Beta Coupé, Fiat Strada, Opel Kadett, VW Golf.

2 Cost considerations
– affordable, or a money pit?

Note: Labour costs will vary greatly
Minor service cost: 6000 miles (10000 kilometres): ●x70-100 approx
Main service cost: 12,000 miles (20,000 kilometres): ●x120-150 approx
New clutch: fitted: parts and labour: ●x200-250 approx
Rebuilt gearbox: parts and labour: ●x1800-2000 approx
Rebuilt engine: parts and labour: ●x1800-2300 approx
Unleaded head conversion: most specialists state that these engines can be run on unleaded fuel without modification
Brake discs: ●x35-50 each approx
Brake pads: ●x25-30 axle set approx
New front wing: ●x200-220
New headlight: ●x70-plus where available
Left-hand drive to right-hand drive conversion: not recommended
Complete body restoration: ●x4000-5000 approx
Full respray including preparation: ●x1800-2500 depending on panel condition
New bodyshell: not available

Parts that are easy to find
Service items; most mechanical parts.

Parts that are difficult to find
Headlights, exterior trim and clips, interior trim and fittings, brake callipers (all models). Sprint body panels.
    The supply situation changes constantly, however.

Headlights are getting hard to find.

Rebuilding the boxer engine is often cheaper than you might think.

3 Living with an Alfasud

– will you get along together?

Good points

Today, owning and driving a 'sud will give you a grin as wide as the Grand Canyon, so accomplished is the little Alfa Romeo's dynamic packaging. Even now, not many cars can claim to offer the driver the same levels of enjoyment as does the Alfasud.

The car's peppy performance from its low-mounted, flat-four 'boxer' engine, its telepathy-like steering and sublime handling all conspire to work in sweet perfunctory harmony, leaving you feeling very happy with the world. Very happy indeed, in fact. So, if you've never actually driven an Alfasud, put it at the top of your 'to-do' list, and prepare to become an addict to family motoring, Italian-style! It's an absolute blast!

Classic profile with large glass areas means great visibility all-round.

So what's all the fuss about? Well, even now, the Alfasud remains a perennial favourite for enthusiastic drivers. Throughout its production life the 'sud received praise for its flat, roll-free cornering, tactile steering, and rasping exhaust note: attributes that are appreciated every bit as much now as they were back in the day, and which meant that all manner of failings could be forgiven. The 'sud was always seen as the dynamic class-leader, historically receiving accolades from drivers, the motoring press, and even other manufacturers. *CAR* magazine once declared it 'The Car of The Decade,' and Ford used it as a bench mark for its front-wheel drive Escort MkIII during the 1980s.

You'll want an Alfasud because there is just so much about the design that was – and still very much is – spot-on. It's a practical little saloon with enough room for the kids or the in-laws, but it doesn't advertise its intrinsic fun quotient – fun that it delivers by the bucket-load, thanks to a lovely rorty exhaust note, tight front-wheel drive handling, quick rack-and-pinion steering, and rapid acceleration coupled with remarkably high levels of refinement for good measure.

Plenty of room for the driver, and passengers, too.

Plenty of boot space for luggage.

Bad points

Build quality was never a strong point on Alfasuds and Sprints, although later models were, thankfully, much improved. Servicing costs are reasonable, though you should always be on the lookout for rust: if you have a garage, use it. Alfasuds are very much revered as drivers' cars, but if you're expecting such modernity as power assisted steering, anti-lock brakes or air-conditioning, then you'll be disappointed, I'm afraid, and the offset pedals can take a little getting used to. Ventilation is good, but the heater is no more than adequate, so you're unlikely to suffer heat rash from driving an Alfasud in low outside temperatures.

Practicalities. Will it suit your lifestyle?

As we've discovered, Alfasuds are sufficiently refined to use as everyday transport, and both passenger and luggage space is excellent.

You should, though, be asking yourself how you intend to use the car. Could you, for example, see yourself using it only on high days and dry days, or would you want to drive it regularly, or even daily? Must it be a fully restored car that has been used only as a 'show pony,' or could you, perhaps, live with the patina of an original, but usable 'sud?

Perhaps you're considering buying a 'sud to restore, in which case, would you want a roadworthy and road-legal car as a running restoration, or one that you could take off the road to carry out a winter rebuild? Finally, and perhaps most importantly, would you be able to garage it?

Decide what it is you want from your Alfasud as this will ultimately lead to the car you want – and the price you want to pay – to reflect its intended use.

If bought as a second car for use in the summer months on sweeping country lanes and back roads, then the Alfasud is definitely for you. There's no better car for driving from A to B – via C, D, and even E – quickly just for the sheer driving pleasure and hell of it. Remember, too, though that, due to its superb refinement, an Alfasud is a car that can quite easily keep up with modern-day traffic, and that longer hauls along motorways and trunk roads can be tackled with ease.

4 Relative values
– which model for you?

Throughout its production life, the Alfasud saloon retained its basic shape and configuration, an attribute it shared with its coupé sister, the Sprint, even though a veritable plethora of engine and trim levels were available throughout its three Series production life.

The Sprint, though, was always offered with a hatchback, while the saloon had a conventional boot (trunk) until it gained a tailgate later in Series III guise, although, through clever design, the addition of the extra aperture resulted in the body shape remaining largely unaltered. This was, however, at the expense of a few more kilos being added to its dry weight, due to the necessary extra reinforcement: essentially an additional box section running at boot (trunk) floor level between the rear wheelarches to provide the extra bracing needed to eliminate flexing of the bodyshell.

Generally speaking, the earliest models of the saloon, regarded by many as the purest form of its design, are the most sought-after. Later models gained plastic trimmings to adorn the bodywork – very much the fashion at the time – which, arguably, blurred its lines rather than accentuated them.

Sprint models follow the same pattern, with early, chrome-bumpered Series I cars considered the ones to have, although, ultimately, it's down to personal taste. Both the saloon and Sprint in their earliest incarnations were pretty basic machines, with little in the way of creature comforts – or even instrumentation. So if you prefer your 'sud to be better equipped, you could save a bit of money and go for a later model.

As well as being manufactured in their home country of Italy, Alfasuds and Sprints were also assembled from CKD (Complete Knock Down) kits supplied by the factory at plants located in the kinder, sunnier climes of South Africa, Malaysia and Malta.

The Alfasud range.

The first Series ti.

Second Series ti.

Series III ti.

Series II Berlina.

Series III Berlina.

The first Series Alfasud Sprint.

A hatchback for the saloon at last!

The face-lifted Series II Alfasud Sprint.

The market has recently seen a trend for these overseas-produced Alfasuds and Sprints, which are becoming more popular and, as a consequence, command a 5 per cent or so price premium over and above European examples.

- 1971 Nov   Launched at Turin
- 1972 Apr   Production starts
- 1973 Jul   UK launch
- 1974 May   2-dr ti added, 5-speed, spoilers, better seats, 68bhp, 99mph, 12.9sec 0-60
- 1977 May   Sprint UK launch, ti 1.3 running gear, 99mph, 13.1sec 0-60; 5-speed gearbox for 4dr 5M
- 1978 Mar   2-dr ti 1.3 now 75bhp 12.1sec 0-60mph; Aug 1286cc option on 4dr
- 1978 May   Series II, improved interior, plus 1351cc 1.3ti, 1490cc 1.5ti (85bhp, 101mph, 10.9sec 0-60)
- 1979 Feb   Sprint upped to 1490cc, twin carbs
- 1980 Sep   UK-only Alfasud TiS introduced and billed as a Special Edition model
- 1980 Jan   Series III, squared headlights, wrapround plastic bumpers; 1.5ti Veloce gets twin carbs, 95bhp, 107mph
- 1981   Hatchback on 3dr
- 1982   Hatchback on 5dr; ti Green Cloverleaf option with 105bhp
- 1982 Nov   UK-only Sprint Speciale introduced and billed as a Special Edition model
- 1983 May   Sprint restyled
- 1984 Mar   Alfasud saloon/hatch production ends
- 1984   Sprint drops Alfasud name; front discs move outboard, rear drums replace discs, tube rear axle replaces pressed steel beam
- 1987   Sprint gets 1712cc 118bhp
- 1989   Sprint production ends

Last of the line. The final Series Alfa Romeo Sprint.

5 Before you view
– be well informed

To avoid a wasted journey – and the disappointment of finding that the car does not match your expectations – it will help if you're very clear about what questions you want to ask before you pick up the telephone. Some of these points might appear basic, but when you're excited about the prospect of buying your dream classic, it's amazing how some of the most obvious things slip the mind ... Also check the current values of the model you are interested in in classic car magazines, which give both a price guide and auction results.

Where is the car?
Is it going to be worth travelling to the next county – or even across a border? A locally-advertised car which may not sound very interesting can add to your knowledge for very little effort, so make a visit; it might even be in better condition than expected.

Dealer or private sale
Establish early on if the car is being sold by its owner or by a trader. A private owner should have all the history, so don't be afraid to ask detailed questions. A dealer may have more limited knowledge of a car's history, but should have *some* documentation. A dealer may offer a warranty/guarantee (ask for a printed copy), and finance.

Cost of collection and delivery
A dealer may well be used to quoting for delivery by car transporter. A private owner may agree to meet you halfway, but only agree to this after you have seen the car at the vendor's address to validate the documents. Conversely, you could meet halfway and agree the sale but insist on meeting at the vendor's address for the handover.

View: when and where
It is always preferable to view at the vendor's home or business premises. In the case of a private sale, the car's documentation should tally with the vendor's name and address. Arrange to view only in daylight, and avoid a wet day. Most cars look better in poor light, or when wet.

Reason for sale
Do make it one of the first questions. Why is the car being sold, and how long has it been with the current owner? How many previous owners?
    Ask if the car is a domestically registered one or an import.

Condition (body/chassis/interior/mechanicals)
Ask for an honest appraisal of the car's condition. Enquire specifically about some of the check items described in Chapter 7.

All-original specification
An original equipment car will invariably be of higher value than a customised or personalised example.

Matching data/legal ownership

Do VIN/chassis, engine numbers and licence plate match the official registration document? Is the owner's name and address recorded in the official registration document?

For those countries that require an annual test of roadworthiness, does the car have a document showing it complies (an MoT certificate in the UK, which can be verified on 0845 600 5977)?

If a smog/emissions certificate is mandatory, does the car have one?

If required, does the car carry a current road fund license/licence plate tag?

Does the vendor own the car outright? Money might be owed to a finance company or bank; the car could even be stolen. Several organisations will supply data on ownership, based on the car's licence plate number, for a fee. Such companies can often also tell you whether the car has been 'written-off' by an insurance company. In the UK these organisations can supply vehicle data –

HPI –   01722 422 422
AA –   0870 600 0836
DVLA – 0870 240 0010
RAC –   0870 533 3660

Other countries will have similar organisations.

Unleaded fuel

If necessary, has the car been modified to run on unleaded fuel? All but the very earliest 'suds can be safely run on unleaded fuel.

Insurance

Check with your existing insurer before setting out as your current policy might not cover you to drive the car if you do purchase it.

How you can pay

A cheque will take several days to clear, and the seller may prefer to sell to a cash buyer. However, a banker's draft (a cheque issued by a bank) is as good as cash, and safer, so contact your bank and become familiar with the practicalities of obtaining one.

Buying at auction?

If the intention is to buy at auction, see Chapter 10 for further advice.

Professional vehicle check (mechanical examination)

There are often marque/model specialists who will undertake professional examination of a vehicle on your behalf. Owners clubs will be able to put you in touch with such specialists.

Other organisations that will carry out a general professional check in the UK are –

AA –   0800 085 3007 (motoring organisation with vehicle inspectors)
ABS – 0800 358 5855 (specialist vehicle inspection company)
RAC – 0870 533 3660 (motoring organisation with vehicle inspectors)

Other countries will have similar organisations.

6 Inspection equipment

– these items will really help

This book
Reading glasses (if you need them for close work)
Magnet (not powerful: a fridge magnet is ideal)
Torch
Probe (a small screwdriver works very well)
Overalls
Mirror on a stick
Digital camera
A friend, preferably a knowledgeable enthusiast

Before you rush out of the door, gather together a few items that will help as you work your way around the car. This book is designed to be your guide at every step, so take it along, and use the check boxes to help you assess each area of the car you're interested in. Don't be afraid to let the seller see you using it.

Take your reading glasses if you need them to read documents, and make close-up inspections.

A magnet will help you check if the car is full of filler, or has fibreglass panels. Use the magnet to sample bodywork areas all around the car, but be careful not to damage the paintwork. Expect to find a little filler here and there, but not whole panels of the stuff. There's nothing wrong with fibreglass panels, but a purist might want the car to be as original as possible. A torch with fresh batteries will be useful for peering into the wheelarches and under the car.

A small screwdriver can be used – with care – as a probe, particularly in the wheelarches and on the underside. With this you should be able to check an area of severe corrosion, but be careful – if it's really bad the screwdriver might go right through the metal!

Be prepared to get dirty. Take along a pair of overalls, if you have them. Fixing a mirror at an angle on the end of a stick may seem odd, but you'll probably need it to check the condition of the underside of the car. It will also help you to peer into some of the important crevices, and you can also use it, together with the torch, along the underside of the sills and on the floor.

If you have the use of a digital camera, take it along so that later you can study some areas of the car more closely. Take a picture of any part of the car that causes you concern, and seek a second opinion.

Ideally, have a friend or knowledgeable enthusiast accompany you; a second opinion is always valuable.

So, after speaking to the vendor and checking all the details given, you decide you want to have a look at the sale car. If it's a private sale, arrange to go and see the vendor at their home so that you can be certain of the address. Neutral ground is often dangerous ...

Evaluate with your head, not your heart!

After a brief examination, during which you'll be able to identify any likely problem areas with the car, you'll be in a position to decide whether you're going to walk away or continue with a more detailed, thorough inspection. Don't let your heart rule your head, though! Alfa Romeos are an evocative and passionate car marque, that can often bring out the romantic in even the most hardened enthusiast: view the car with both eyes wide open.

Would you know what version of the boxer engine this is just by looking?

In their day, Alfasuds and Sprints were untouchable in terms of dynamic qualities, and unrivalled levels of mechanical grip and refinement. Don't let your vision of enjoying a blast through country lanes with the engine at full chat cloud your judgement. Let your head take the lead!

As a rule, most Alfasuds these days tend to be enthusiast-owned, and therefore well-maintained. There will inevitably be exceptions, though. Anyone trying to run the car on a budget may well have skimped on important and essential maintenance, so be wary. Remember, though, that in the case of the Alfasud and Sprint, a sound-bodied car with suspect or tired mechanicals will always be better in the long run than one with, say, a rebuilt engine but neglected bodywork.

Alfasuds and Sprints can rust just about anywhere.

Look for the best that you can afford, and keep in mind that it's always going to be cheaper to pay a fair price for a good original or restored car, than pay a lower price for a car that obviously requires work. Although the network of Alfasud specialists these days has ensured that parts availability has improved, if you spot anything during your first viewing that'll need putting right, it's likely to be expensive. You have been warned!

Know what you're looking for

As mentioned in Chapter 6, if this is going to be a first-time purchase and you're not familiar with the model, it's always a good idea to ask a friend or colleague who owns an Alfasud or Sprint to come and see the car with you. This is where being a member of an owner's club will be a definite advantage (you can find contact details in Chapter 16: The Alfasud Community). Many clubs have dedicated Alfasud model registers, listing those who can give advice.

Firstly, and this may sound obvious, be sure you know what it is you're looking at. The Alfasud and Sprint range throughout its production life took on a whole raft of guises, and was offered with a wide range of engine options. Although in many respects the engines look similar outwardly, as we've seen in Chapter 4, the flat-four motor was offered in many states of capacity, tune, and power output. A common modification is to replace the 1.2 or 1.3 versions of the engines originally fitted with the higher performance 1.5 or 1.7 boxer units. Some (late model) cars have had the standard equipment, long-ratio gearbox replaced by the early close-ratio version, as, arguably, this results in stronger acceleration at the expense of outright top speed. Again, as with the boxer engines, because of external similarities, it's not possibe to visually identify the type of gearbox. Be certain, therefore, that you familiarise yourself with the technical specifications given in Chapter 4 to avoid buying a car with an identity crisis. It's difficult to tell, even during the test drive, whether the car is fitted with the right engine and transmission combination.

Any combination of engine and transmission is, in fact, possible due to ease of inter-changeability, but the quality of workmanship of such a transplant can, and does, vary. Many vendors will mention in their advertisements if a larger engine or early close-ratio gearbox have been installed, believing it to be a selling point. So, if

Probably needs nothing more than a polish with T-Cut!

you do discover that this is the case, don't be afraid to ask the seller for details, and evidence of who carried out the work and the relative condition of the donor units: where they came from, in other words. It's vitally important that any paperwork accompanying the car reflects the inclusion of a non-standard transplanted engine or transmission, and, if you do decide to go ahead with the purchase, for goodness' sake make certain that you arrange insurance for the vehicle's *exact* specification, otherwise you may find the cover is invalid.

Chassis number stamped on bulkhead (firewall).

It's unusual, unless the car's owner is a stickler for originality, to find a car that doesn't have one or more non-standard features, even if it's only a different set of alloy wheels, or, internally, an aftermarket steering wheel, so be prepared to accept and adapt to these compromises.

In the UK, conversions from left-hand drive to right hand drive on the Alfasud and Sprint are virtually unheard of, although, occasionally, you can come across 'left-hooker' imports. Having benefited from

VIN (Vehicle Identification Number) plate on inner wing panel in engine bay.

sunnier and thus drier climes means that there are some very sound examples of both the Alfasud and Sprint, so it's currently becoming progressively more popular to import a first-rate example. This being the case, be aware that specifications vary from market to market. With South Africa being the most common place to source your import, make sure that you know what it is you're looking at – see Chapter 4 – and try and find out about any work that's been carried out.

Whether import or domestic, when it comes to the Alfasud and Sprint, a standard specification car is always going to be worth more than a modified one. Don't discount modified vehicles, though; just make certain you know the quality and extent of the work carried out. You only have yourself to blame if you don't …

Legalities

At this stage ask to see the car's official registration document (Log Book, Pink Slip, V5 or equivalent) to verify not only the present owner's name and address and the vehicle's licence plate number, but also the car's chassis or VIN number, its make and model and, perhaps, the date of first registration. Don't be shy about asking to see the vendor's proof of identity, their legal entitlement to sell the car, and the car's certificate of roadworthiness (MoT in the UK), or, if applicable, proof of its SORN (Statutory Off Road Notification), otherwise a fine will be due.

The procedures involved in importing a car first registered abroad are complex, so it's important to ask if the relevant process has been followed, otherwise you could end up with a bill from Customs or, ultimately, have the car impounded until all duties are paid, with the prospect of losing the car altogether if the fees aren't paid on time! The car may not even be registered in your country, so, for peace of mind, consider consulting a specialist to ensure that everything is in order.

Do try and keep the registration documents to hand so that you can check the numbers under the bonnet (hood) when you're looking over the car's mechanical components. Make a note of them, and any other relevant details.

Exterior

What are you looking for here? Simple: rust! There aren't many Alfasuds or Sprints around nowadays that haven't had either a total or partial respray, so please refer to Chapter 14 for pointers and notes on paint finishes. Rust can break out almost anywhere on these cars because, as we've learned, rust-proofing when the car was new was virtually non-existent, particularly on the earliest cars. It doesn't help here that Alfa Romeo's idea of rust-proofing on later cars was to fill cavities with foam, which simply absorbed moisture, resulting in many panels rotting from the inside-out.

So, from the onset, ask whether any bodywork restoration has been carried out, and, if so, by whom and when? Be wary if it turns out that the work has been done by a non-Alfa Romeo specialist: during their lifetime, many cars suffered less-than-perfect repairs in order to move them on. As we've already said, beware of previous poor bodywork repairs or restoration as rampant rust may well resurface.

Because of the poor quality, Soviet-sourced, recycled steel used on early variants, corrosion can break out almost anywhere on some or all of the outer panels because of impurities in the metal. With this in mind, you can now begin your systematic walk around the car, looking for signs of rust or bubbling paintwork. Don't be tempted to do this if it's raining, though, or when the light is not good.

Beginning at the front of the car, look at the leading edge of the bonnet (hood), which may have stone chips that will rust if left untreated and not touched in. The front outer wings often show signs of corrosion along their top edges, and around the wheelarches if they haven't been replaced in the past with fibreglass items, which is common. Next, closely inspect the front windscreen surround and A-posts. This was one of the areas where Alfa Romeo used injected foam to 'rust-proof' the panels, so be on the lookout for severe corrosion or signs of previous poor repairs.

Run your hand over the doors to check for rust spots, and visually inspect the rear wheelarches, which should have no bubbling paintwork or evidence of previous poor repairs.

At the rear of the car, if it's a booted model you're looking at, take a note of the condition of the external boot (trunk) lid hinges, which can seize, resulting in a difficult repair. Later models received plastic mouldings to cover the hinges and protect them from the worst of the weather, but the hinges can still corrode. While you're there, inspect the condition of the rear screen surround. If there's rust here the screen will have to come out in order to repair satisfactorily. Check the boot (trunk) lid for signs of rust, particularly at the window surround. If it's a hatchback version you're looking at, similar inspections apply. Again, any corrosion spotted around the rear screen will mean it'll have to come out in order to repair the aperture properly. Remember that the rear boot (trunk) lid – or hatchback on later models – can only be opened from inside the car by means of cable operation, via a lever beside the front seats, so check this works.

Check the boot (trunk) lid or tailgate slam panel. Raise the boot lid (or tailgate, depending on model), lift the floor covering and check the floor and spare wheel well for rust or signs of previous repairs. Ripples or distortions here will mean it's possible that the car has had a rear end collision, and been repaired. Check that the spare wheel and tyre are present and correct.

On two- and three-door versions of the 'sud or Sprint, carefully inspect the rear side window surrounds, as these can hide rust that has occurred due to the drain holes or tubes becoming blocked or damaged. As you make your way along the car's sides, look for rust spreading from various fixing points in doors or panels penetrated by fixings for door mirrors or side protection panels. Run your hand over the roof to check for any corrosion on the panel in general, but particularly around the aperture for the sunroof, if the car has one.

At the front of the car once more, raise the bonnet (hood) and check the chassis rails in the engine bay for rust. Look also at the front bulkhead (which should be corrosion-free), and the battery tray behind the bulkhead. Acid spills from the battery can strip the paint, exposing bare metal and resulting in more rust.

As a final check top-side of the car, examine the sides of the car for rippling or creasing, which could indicate poor accident repair. Do this by crouching down at each corner in turn, and looking along the car's flanks each side. Check, too, that the body shut gaps are equal all round, plus the condition of any brightwork or badges.

Now it's time to get down and dirty as we make the all-important check of the car's underside. If you have access to a lift or ramps, then all well and good, but, if not, don't be afraid to lay on the floor using your torch and probe to help carry out the inspection.

Working from the front of the car backward, have a look (which may be just a cursory glance on some later models due to their having chin spoilers fitted as standard) at the front valance. Next, see if you can get under the front wings to check the condition of the inner wing panels, and, while there, inspect the area to the rear of the front wheelarches/base of the A-posts: a known rust spot. Continuing towards the rear of the car, check the sills on both sides (again, maybe no more than a cursory glance for later models, as they have plastic sill mouldings fitted as standard, which can hide the sills' true condition). If you can, carefully run a gloved finger or two under the plastic trim, to check if the sill itself feels solid or whether you can feel any rust-bubbling, or even holes, in the metal. Look also at the floorpan as rust spots can appear anywhere here, due to poor rust-proofing. Finally, at the back of the car, check the condition of the rear chassis outriggers and suspension mounts, inspecting also the pressed steel rear beam axle, as this is another component that can rust from the inside-out. Finish off by checking the rear valance for rust.

As we've said, bodywork repairs are almost certainly going to be much more expensive to carry out properly than nearly every other repair that may be necessary. Having completed your external inspection, and having established that you don't want a restoration project, if you've not been put off thus far, we'll move on to the inside ...

Interior

A generally musty smell emanating from the car's interior indicates damp, caused either by blocked drainage holes or channels, or worse – as I have seen – gaping holes in the floorpan! Ask the seller to lift the floor covering or carpets to check for damp, which should not be visible, and neither, too, should the road beneath the car! A number of drain plugs in the Alfasud/Sprint floorpan are retained by rubber grommets. Over time, the rubber can perish, allowing moisture to penetrate and lead to rust around the drain holes. In the worst case scenario, the plug falls out completely, following which an ever-increasing-in-size hole appears in the floor! With the carpet up, check also for corrosion around the pedal assembly on the bulkhead. If problems exist with the floorpan, welded repairs can be carried out by plating the holes or, in some cases, replacing a whole (excuse the pun) section with a pre-fabricated panel.

The material used to trim the seats on the Alfasud and Sprint can be prone to splitting, and finding good quality used replacement seats is becoming difficult. Trying to find new fabric for repairs is similarly difficult, although, with the resurgence in popularity of the 'sud range, model enthusiasts at car clubs or online specialist suppliers have been known to start remanufacturing the material.

Next, have a quick look at the dashboard, the top padding of which can split due to exposure to sunlight, and check that all of the instruments and gauges are present and work correctly, and then check the steering wheel and gear knob for signs of serious wear, which can indicate that the car's had a hard life. Finally, look up at the headlining to check for tears or rips, and that it's stain-free, particularly around the sunroof aperture if the car is so equipped.

Mechanical
Pop the bonnet (hood) now and check the general appearance of the engine. Alfa Romeo certainly knows how to produce some good-looking motors, and the flat-four boxer unit used in the Alfasud range is no exception. Generally, a clean engine bay gives an indication of the car's overall level of care. A grubby, tired-looking engine bay can be a real let-down.

Check the engine and chassis/VIN numbers against those given in the car's registration documents. The engine number is stamped on the lower block on the fuel pump side of the engine bay, whilst the VIN number is stamped into the car's bulkhead on the left-hand side of the car, looking from the front.

Next, pull out the oil dipstick and check the level and condition of the engine oil. Dirty oil and a low level could be a sign of neglect, so ask the owner when the oil was last changed. With the engine cold, remove the expansion tank cap and check for sludge around the filler neck and inside the cap itself, as this could indicate head gasket problems. Look, too, at the coolant levels, and try and establish if there's any anti-freeze in the coolant (usually visible by its colour). Cloudy, murky brown-coloured coolant generally points to a lack of care.

At this point, ask the seller to start the engine for you. The flat-four motor should start either first or second throw, with or without the use of the choke. You're not after a test drive at this stage, but merely ensuring that the engine runs smoothly when idling, and is free from coolant leaks. Look under the car while the engine is idling to check for oil or fuel drips. Once at operating temperature, the thermostatically-controlled electric cooling fan should cut in.

Finally (for now), push down on each corner of the car and release, checking for smooth operation of the shock absorbers and listening for any creaks or squeaks. Overall, the car should sit level and straight, with any sagging evident usually the result of tired springs.

Is it worth staying for a closer look?
Do you feel that the car is basically sound, requiring little or no attention? Are you able, in terms of time and expense involved, to take on a rolling restoration? If the car is going to be fully restored, do you feel you have, or know someone who has, the skills and expertise to complete the job at reasonable cost?

Following your 15-minute inspection, and after asking yourself the above questions, you should be in a position to either walk away or stay to make a more detailed inspection. If you haven't walked away by now, then it's time for a cup of tea, if it's on offer, before continuing with a more thorough assessment of the car's condition.

8 Key points
– where to look for problems

Rot spots
- Chassis rails in engine bay
- Inner wings, steering rack mountings
- Rear of front wheelarches inner/outer, front bulkhead
- Front screen surround, A-posts
- Floorpans
- Sills
- Rear screen surround/pillars inc rear side windows 2-3 door)
- Rear chassis outriggers/suspension mounts
- Boot floor and spare wheel well
- All outer panels – valances, wings, doors, hatches, lids, roof

Rear of front wheelarches should be inspected carefully.

Severe corrosion of the chassis rails in the engine bay makes the car a scrapper.

Inner wings should be rust-free.

Front A-post and windscreen surround should be in good order.

Floorpans should be corrosion-free.

Sills, ideally, should not have holes in them!

Rear suspension mounts should be solid.

Water ingress here around the rear side windows spells trouble.

Boot (trunk) floor and spare wheel well should ideally look like this.

Check all outer panels for rot!

Score each section using the boxes as follows:
4 = Excellent; 3 = Good; 2 = Average; 1 = Poor
The totting-up procedure is detailed at the end of the chapter. Be realistic in your marking!

Having made it this far – and, hopefully, feeling refreshed after your post-fifteen minute evaluation cup of tea – armed with your inspection equipment (see Chapter 6) you can begin to assess the car more seriously. Allow up to an hour for this systematic examination, broken down into three parts: assessment of the exterior bodywork and interior; the underside (a ramp check is the ideal) and, finally, a test drive of at least fifteen minutes if the car is a runner and road-legal, and your insurance allows it. A top tip here is to use a magnet to check for filler in the metalwork.

Exterior
General   4️⃣ 3️⃣ 2️⃣ 1️⃣

Bodywork condition is far more important than the car's mechanical state, as virtually all service parts are readily available, meaning that the majority of mechanical tasks are straightforward to deal with. Some good quality steel body repair panels are available from a network of specialists, and some even supply whole, good, rust-free, used repair sections salvaged from scrap cars. Fibreglass panels such as front wings, rear quarters, spoilers, bonnets (hoods) and tailgates are available, too, which, although not appealing to the purist, do eradicate the threat of rust, and are very lightweight. Use the tickbox to indicate your first impression of how the car presents.

Bodywork restoration is likely to be labour-intensive and expensive.

Paintwork ☒4 ☒3 ☒2 ☒1

Unless the car has very recently been fully restored, you should expect imperfections in the paintwork of some kind or other. It is likely that a full or partial respray, sometimes of dubious quality, has been carried out on the car at some point in its life. Chapter 14 shows you how to identify paintwork problems.

Wheels ☒4 ☒3 ☒2 ☒1

The wheels fitted to Alfasuds or Sprints can be of several different designs, and either steel or alloy in construction. Check that they're all of the same design and type on the car, and carefully evaluate their condition, and for buckling/kerb damage. Check that the wheel centres are all present and correct on alloy wheels, as good secondhand replacements are phenomenally expensive.

Check wheels and tyres for condition and uniformity.

Tyres ☒4 ☒3 ☒2 ☒1

Ideally, all of the tyres fitted to the car will be of the same make and pattern. Different types and makes of tyre should never be fitted across either the front or rear axles, as this can upset the car's handling: fit tyres as axle sets. Check overall condition; also for age-related cracking on the sidewalls, and bulges.

Lights ☒4 ☒3 ☒2 ☒1

Establish that these all work. Carefully check the condition of all light lenses for cracking and damage from stone chips. On headlights, in particular, look for signs of internal corrosion or lifting of the silvering on the reflectors, as this can seriously reduce their efficiency.

Check all lights for operation and condition.

The round headlights of the ti models are now virtually extinct, which could be an issue if replacement is needed. Even when they're in perfect condition, compared to present-day cars, the Alfasud's and Sprint's headlights will appear less efficient, although output can be increased by fitting uprated modern proprietary bulbs.

Badges and trim ☒4 ☒3 ☒2 ☒1

Check that all of the exterior trim and badges are present and correct. Good trim, and new or good used badges are becoming difficult to find, as are trim retaining clips, although many specialists have begun to remanufacture some types using 3D printer technology.

Make sure that all external badges and trim are present. Replacements are scarce and expensive.

Interior
Floor  ④ ③ ② ①
During our fifteen minute evaluation, hopefully, you'll have satisfied yourself that floor condition isn't too bad, so now you need to investigate further by taking a little more time with this, lifting carpets, checking again for dampness, and inspecting as much of the floor as possible, including where it meets the inner sills.

Carpets ④ ③ ② ①
Take a close look at the carpets to check for rips, splits and discolouration. Replacement carpet sets are available but are becoming pricey. Also check the felt underlay for condition and signs of dampness. If allowed to get wet, the underlay will retain water like a sponge, leading to corrosion of the floor panel, so

Check carpets and floor coverings. The rubber mat flooring from the earliest models is now extremely hard to find.

check this is dry and intact. Very early basic 'suds had rubber mats to cover the floor, and the same inspection procedure applies here, in the knowledge that new rubber floor covering sections are now virtually unobtainablc.

Pedals ④ ③ ② ①
The 'long arms and short legs' driving position in the Alfasud and Sprint will be noticeable, especially when compared to a modern car, as will the offset pedals, but you can get used to this in time. The pedals are also quite close to one another, so drivers with broad feet should be careful not to press two at the same time. Check the condition of the pedal rubbers, and also that they are secure. Replacement pedal rubbers are becoming difficult to find.

Seats ④ ③ ② ①
Take time to establish seat condition, many incarnations of which were fitted to the Alfasud and Sprint model range during its production life. Check that all the

Replacement seats, material, interior trim and doorcards are becoming rare so check for damage.

adjusters and runners work as they should, and also that the seatback release catch (on two- and three-door models) engages and locks properly.

Seat material has been unobtainable for many years, so if repair is needed, you'll have to visit a specialist car trimmer to see what can be done (although replica seat cloth is being remanufactured by many enthusiast clubs on a very small scale). It'll be a costly exercise, whichever way you go.

Door cards

Carefully check for overall condition and signs of damage. Door cards should be straight and not warped, which is an indication of moisture ingress. Good condition replacement trim is expensive, and difficult to source.

Window operation

Window winders should work freely, so beware any stiffness in their operation. The electric windows found on some later, more plush, models should operate smoothly, and open and close the door glass without judder. The rear windows on two- and three-door models open for ventilation (see the inspection procedure later in this chapter).

Headlining

This should be sag- and rip-free, and clean. Water stains can be removed, but check carefully around the aperture for the sunroof (if fitted) as water trapped here is going to lead to serious problems down the line. Replacement headlining is scarce, and difficult to fit properly.

See that the headlining is undamaged and stain-free particularly around the sunroof aperture.

Bodywork
Front and rear valances

The front and rear valances below the bumpers can rot away completely. What makes this harder to spot is the black plastic mouldings used as standard on later cars to effectively enclose these areas, meaning rust can go undetected for some while. Although the resultant corrosion damage is obviously unsightly, detracting from the car's overall appearance, the front valance does, to an extent, protect

Check condition of front and rear valances carefully.

the suspension subframe with its anti-roll bar attachment points mounted immediately behind it. These can be more thoroughly inspected when you're under the car. Valance repair sections are no longer available, so to repair effectively, you're looking at having to replace the complete front or rear panels with NOS (New Old Stock), or good, used items from a donor car.

Wings (fenders)

These can rust along their top edge, around the wheelarch (particularly if it's a late model car with plastic wheelarch extensions that can trap moisture), at the front lower section around the bumper mounting, and particularly at the lower rear section behind the front wheel, forward of the A-post. None of this necessarily needs to be a problem, as replacement steel – and even fibreglass wings and front and rear steel repair sections – can be sourced, but it's what's going on *behind* the outer wing (fender) that's considerably more important; it's vital to check (see Ramp Check pages later in this chapter).

Condition of the front wings (fenders) is important as they may hide all sorts of horrors beneath.

Front screen surround and A-posts

All Alfasuds and Sprints can rot here. Screen surround sections are no longer available, so rust damage or holes in either the screen corners or screen apertures must be repaired using hand-fabricated and contoured metalwork, which can be expensive. If you are fortunate enough to locate a NOS repair section, please note that the panel profiles for the Berlina and Sprint are slightly different, so aren't interchangeable. Do check carefully for evidence of previous repairs. It's not uncommon for these areas to have been patched up using only body filler, so use your magnet to check. Very early Series I cars had bonded windscreens, and very often the screen aperture was left untreated – or even unpainted – at the factory, exposing bare metal before the glass was bonded into position, allowing rust to spread uncontrollably. Remember, too, that although rust-proofing applied at the factory improved markedly from the 1980 model year, the A-post and screen surround was one of the places on the car that Alfa Romeo 'improved' by injecting foam into closed sections, which only made things worse, so take your time checking out this area.

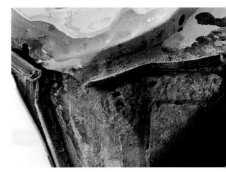

This type of corrosion damage to the front windscreen surround an A-post is not uncommon.

Doors

Have a closer look now to check whether the doors are square in their aperture, and that panel gaps are equal all the way round. Make a note, too, of whether the doors open and close easily, and fit flush on their latches. The front doors on two- or three-door 'suds and Sprints are fairly long and heavy

Door bottoms rust out. Poor repairs like this are typical, although new repair panels are available.

in comparison to those on the four- or five-door Berlinas, so check that they don't sag on their hinges. Check door bottoms for rust and blocked drain holes. If the drain holes are blocked, it's likely that moisture has been collecting inside the doors, which leads to corrosion of the door bottoms.

Have a close look, too, at the condition of the door skins. Use your magnet to check for filler, and take a close look at the attachment points of door mirrors – and body side protection panels on later model Sprints – to check whether corrosion has affected any of the holes penetrating the skin. Check at the top of the door frames for rust: if there is any it will usually be only surface rust, but if there's serious rot, the door will need replacing. It's not all bad news: repair sections for the door bottoms of all models are available, as, too, are NOS, or complete sound used doors.

Check the rubber seals around the door apertures for splits or perishing, which will allow the ingress of rainwater, and cause unnecessary wind noise.

Rear side windows on the two- or three-door cars

The rear side windows open on both types of the Alfasud bodyshell, saloon and coupé, but the operating mechanism varies. On the Berlina, the rear window is simply hinged at the B-post, and opens outwards at the rear. Check that this works; that the hinges haven't come away from the B-post, and that the frame around the glass is rust-free.

On the Sprint, the rear windows are designed to drop down from the top a

Water ingress to the rear side windows can cause damage, much of it hidden like this rotted metal channel.

On Sprints the only option is a tricky and expensive repair to the window regulators. Note reinstatement of the drain tube.

The Sprint's B-post covers can rot from the inside out.

couple of inches (50cm) for ventilation, and are operated by a knob on the inside of the car. Check that they work: they often don't. A tip here is to pour some water down the side windows and watch for it being expelled from the outlet pipe just in front of the rear wheels.

There's a drain pipe located in the base of the window winder mechanism at each side of the car, which is designed to carry away rainwater, clear of the regulators to prevent ingress. If it's blocked or has become detached, moisture won't be discharged via the drain tubes as it should, and will become trapped in the regulator housings, rusting-out the regulator, and causing it to completely seize and become inoperable.

Even worse, any rainwater that enters the car can then simply collect in the sill bottom and potentially rot it out, so make extra careful checks here. It's all repairable – but at a cost. As with the Berlina, make a thorough check of the side window frame.

On Sprint models, the B-posts have painted metal trim panels as embellishment. These can rot out from the inside (identified by bubbling paint), so inspect carefully as replacements are becoming hard to find.

Rear quarter panels and pillars

Now is the time to look again at the car's rear quarter panels: this time in more detail. Due to the impurities present in the low-grade recycled steel used in the 'sud's early life, rust can break out just about anywhere, so you'll need your magnet to check for filler. Check, too, for bubbling around the rear wheelarches as this can be a portent of something more serious. Later Series cars, with their black plastic wheelarch extensions, can hide some serious corrosion, so pay particular attention to this area, too.

The good news is that replacement steel wheelarch repair sections, and, indeed, complete NOS (New Old Stock) steel rear quarter panels are available if you know where to look. Failing that, if you're not particularly bothered about originality, full quarter panels are available in fibreglass, although it might be worth checking with your insurance company whether your cover will be affected if you go this route. Don't forget to examine the fuel filler flap, and the area around the filler cap, for rust: a tricky repair.

Check all over the rear quarter panels and wheelarches for rust damage.

Sills

Tap the sills with the handle of a small screwdriver all along their length. You should hear a clean, metallic noise if the panels are sound. A dull-sounding resonance probably indicates corrosion within the closed cavities, or even that the closed cavity is full of water!

Boot (trunk) hatch or lid and rear screen

All three Series of the Alfasud Berlina were available with a boot (trunk), and were unusual in that the lid had externally mounted hinges and no stay, which meant that the boot (trunk) lid rests on the rear window when in fully opened position! Because of the vulnerable, open-to-the-elements external hinge placement, many owners found that, once the hinges had seized, the lid could literally fall or snap off, so make certain that the hinges have received regular lubrication to ensure smooth operation. Ascertain, too, that the lid slam panel is corrosion-free, as drain holes have been known to become blocked, allowing rainwater to stand in the panel and cause rust. Check that the aperture lip is in good condition, and that the rubber seal surround is doing its job of keeping out water.

Rusting out of the tailgate here suggests that the drain holes are blocked or the drain tubes are missing.

Take another look now at the rear screen and its surrounds. Gently run your finger nail around the rubber seal to lift it slightly. Rust bubbles found here on the screen aperture are bad news, as the glass will have to come out in order to achieve a satisfactory repair.

Later models of the Berlina and the Sprint had a hatchback, and generally the same inspection procedures relating to the aperture, rubber seal and rear screen surround apply. The tailgate slam panels require special attention as they incorporate drainage tubes designed to prevent rainwater from standing in the panel and causing corrosion damage: check whether these are blocked – or even missing completely!

Of special note is that the rear light clusters of later Series III saloons extended into either the boot (trunk) lid or hatchback, so electrical power for the reversing lights and rear fog lights (and optional rear wiper motor and heated rear screen element on the hatchbacks), was provided by way of a contact plate on the lid (or tailgate) slam panel coming into contact with the spring-loaded brass 'fingers' mounted to the underside of the lid (or tailgate) when in the closed position. Check whether these are operational otherwise the lights (and rear wiper, if fitted) will not function. Check carefully, too, that the pipe for the rear screen wash is intact and in position on hatchback models.

Spare wheel well

You'll have already had a cursory glance at the boot (trunk) floor during your earlier fifteen minute evaluation, but now it's time to take a closer look at the spare wheel well.

Remove the spare wheel and tyre and inspect

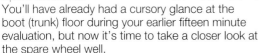

With the spare wheel out, check the wheel well for signs of damage or previous repairs. Check also the boot (trunk) rear crossmember for corrosion (structural).

the spare wheel well panel for signs of rust and previous repairs, particularly around the drain plug mounted at the bottom of the well. The drain plug is retained by way of a rubber grommet. Over time, the rubber deteriorates, allowing moisture to penetrate, and leading to the outbreak of rust around the drain hole. In the worst case, the plug falls out, following which, a hole, ever-increasing in size, appears in the well!

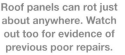

Roof panels can rot just about anywhere. Watch out too for evidence of previous poor repairs.

Roof

Historically, the steel used to form the Alfasud's body panels was of very questionable quality. Rust can break out just about anywhere due to the impurities present in the recycled metal, and this is especially so on the larger bodywork panels such as the roof, so very carefully check its surface for any sign of corrosion or previous repairs. Use your magnet to check for filler, and look for rust spreading from the top edge of the front windscreen, and around the top of the rear screen or hatchback, depending on model. It would probably be best to repair any corrosion to the leading and trailing edges of the roof panel with complete used, sound, rust-free sections. If the car is fitted with a sunroof, check very carefully for paint bubbles around its aperture.

Bonnet (hood) and engine bay

The same rule applies to the bonnet (hood) panel in that rust can break out just about anywhere on its surface. The front leading edge of the bonnet (hood) can take a battering, and suffer from stone chips, so check very carefully for signs of damage here. With the bonnet (hood) raised – all Alfasud and Sprint bonnets (hoods) are forward-opening – check that the hinges are sound, and that they aren't coming away from the hinge crossmember. Check, too, that the bonnet (hood) stays work freely and are not missing: a common problem. On the underside of the bonnet (hood) panel, check for rust bubbles appearing around the inner steel strengthening webbing.

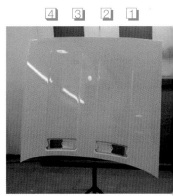

The bonnet (hood), shown here removed from the car, should be checked for rust and previous repairs.

The front bulkhead, shown here with the engine removed, should be inspected carefully. Light surface rust such as this is okay; holes are not! Note steering rack mountings and bushes.

Behind the front bulkhead (firewall) check for rust around the battery tray.

On the other side, look for rust around and under the brake servo.

Closely examine the chassis mounting rails at the top of the inner wings (fenders).

In the engine bay, look very closely at the chassis rails running down both sides of the engine. It's imperative that you establish the condition of these rails – check using the 'sound test' by tapping a small screwdriver handle along their length, listening for any dull resonance as previously described. Repairs needed here are difficult and very expensive, and could even be a deal-breaker.

Behind the bulkhead (firewall) have a closer look at the area around the battery tray, and inspect for rust damage. On the other side, thoroughly inspect the metal under the brake servo unit for signs of corrosion damage: a tricky and time-consuming repair. Check that the drain holes are clear and show no sign of corrosion.

Ramp check
Underbody (general)   4 3 2 1

Having satisfied yourself that you have a seriously good idea of what kind of shape the car is in bodywork-wise top side, it's now time now to thoroughly inspect the car's underside for signs of corrosion damage or previous repairs. If you or the seller have access to a ramp, this is ideal for carrying out this inspection. If not, you may have to lie on your back and get under the car, with your torch and other inspection equipment to hand. Look over all parts of the floorpan and check on the condition of the metal brake and petrol pipes. Carefully inspect the exhaust system for condition. Check also that the fuel tank shows no sign of leaking.

Check underbody for general condition.

Underbody (rear) ④ ③ ② ①

Next, check the condition of the rear chassis outriggers and suspension mounts. Any corrosion here will affect the safety of the car, and is tricky to put right. Whilst there, check the condition of the rear beam axle, particularly around the spring seatings, which is also an obvious safety concern. The metal can also crack at the shock absorber (damper) and tie rod attachment points due to metal fatigue. Don't worry unduly if this is the case, as replacement used beam axles are available, with some being galvanised to protect from further corrosion. Check that all of the rubber bushes are intact on the tie-bars and linkages. It's not a difficult job in itself to replace these, but it can be a very time-consuming one. Shine your torch up into the rear inner wheelarches, and have a good look for any rust. Your torch should also be in action again as you inspect the condition of the rubber downpipe that runs from the fuel filler cap neck to the fuel tank itself. Check on the condition of any flexible brake system hoses at the rear axle, which should be free from leakages, bulges and perishing.

Check all suspension attachment points, all rubber bushes, brake and petrol pipes, condition of rear beam axle (galvanised item fitted here) and rubber downpipe into fuel tank.

Underbody (front and sides) ④ ③ ② ①

Working towards the front of the car from the back, check the sills for holes or corrosion, particularly along their inside edges where they meet the floorpan. Replacement panels are available, but repairs can be expensive. Inspect the front and rear jacking points. They should be in good condition.

At the front of the car below the bulkhead (firewall), use your torch to check the condition of the steering rack mountings and their bushes. Any attention needed here ideally requires the engine and gearbox to come out for better access.

Have a good look, too, at the front suspension and subframe mountings. Check also on the condition of the front and rear suspension arms and, at the very front of the car behind the front valance, the condition of the front anti-roll bar attachment points and their bushes. Any play in the bushes will mean a general sloppiness when

Have a good poke around the rear suspension and tie-bar mountings.

Look closely at the front suspension arms, check for any play at their bushes and inspect fuel and brake pipes.

The front inner wing panels (shown here with dampers removed) should look like this, and be intact with no rust holes.

driving the car. The suspension arms are fabricated from pressed metal extrusions, creating closed cavities that can rust; again, NOS replacements are available with some being galvanised. Check on the condition of any flexible brake system hoses, which should be free from leakages, bulges or perishing.

With the engine warm, check the condition of the engine and gearbox mounts by rocking the engine unit, and looking for excess movement.

Underbody (front inner wings)

Fair warning here: this area can be a mess in terms of corrosion damage, and, although not entirely impossible to repair, can be a bit of a money pit to put right. Due to a design fault, water and any debris thrown up by the front road wheels collects in the recess behind the wheelarches in front of the A-posts. Rust can then spread from here, along the front inner wings and front wing attachment rails. None of these panels is readily available, and are now out of production, so any work will necessitate using one-off, hand-fabricated repair sections, which will be costly unless you're handy with the welding torch ...

If you're unlucky, this is what you'll find hidden behind the outer wings (fenders).

Test drive
Start-up

Having come this far, if the car is a runner and road-legal, and your insurance allows it, you'll now want to take it for a test drive. So, sit in the driver's seat, and make yourself comfortable whilst checking the condition and operation of the seat belts. Build quality was never the best on Alfasuds and Sprints, so expect the odd shake, rattle and roll when on the move!

An Alfasud should start at the first or second attempt with or without the manual choke, and then idle smoothly. It's common for the carburettor(s) to have been 'fiddled' with, especially on twin carb versions, where they are not quite balanced correctly, leading to rough running. Puffs of smoke on start-up and on the overrun indicate worn valve guides. A rumble from the bottom of the engine may be a worn water pump. To identify this, with the engine stopped, rock the water pump's pulley and check for any up-and-down or side-to-side movement, indicating worn bearings within the pump assembly.

Clutch and transmission

Check the operation of the clutch pedal. All Alfasuds run hydraulic clutches, so if the pedal's not smooth in operation, or you experience 'judder,' suspect a leak in the hydraulic system, with the slave cylinder being the chief culprit: an easy fix. Don't worry about clutch 'chatter.' They (really do) all do that!

On the move, gear changes should be tight and precise. If they're not, the gearlever bushes will need replacing: a common fault. Also check the synchromesh on second gear. If this is really bad, you'll need to fit either a secondhand exchange or rebuilt gearbox. A grumbling noise on the move may be due to damaged differential gears.

Warning lights

It's not unusual for the carburettors to have been fiddled with, resulting in poor running.

The car should reach operating temperature pretty quickly, so keep an eye on the temperature gauge (if fitted). If the red coolant warning light on the dashboard comes on in normal driving conditions, stop the car immediately to investigate this, as the engine is about to overheat. The alternator warning light should go off immediately after the car is started, so if it flickers or comes on permanently when driving, this probably means that the alternator is on its way out or, if you're lucky, the fan belt needs adjustment.

Braking system

Check that all warning lights and gauges work correctly. Noise at speedo head indicates an issue with the cable.

The brakes should pull up the car squarely and evenly, so if there's a tendency to lock up or the brakes aren't efficieint in some way, this will need looking at, and probably indicates sticking or seized brake callipers. Unusually, unless you're driving a Series III Sprint, the handbrake on the Alfasud works on the front wheels, so check for its efficacy, as poor operation is likely to be caused by issues at the calliper end, with either the cable being miss-adjusted or the handbrake pivot on the calliper body may have become seized. Check that oil from the engine or gearbox isn't getting onto the inboard front brakes. Poor adjustment after pad replacement, and poor handbrake setup, are common, and can be fixed.

Ride and suspension

The Alfasud's handling and ride is renowned for its refinement, so, if you detect a feeling of vagueness, or the car feels a little wallowy, suspect worn suspension bushes. Unless you intend to go racing, resist the temptation (and the expense) to fit aftermarket hard Polyurethane bushes rather than OE (Original Equipment) items, as they simply don't have the compliance of the rubber originals, and you'll lose some of the car's legendary roadholding proficiency as a result. Most notably, the rear suspension bushes were always meant to be soft in nature, leading to a degree of designed-in 'rear-wheel-steer' that further contributes to the car's overall handling prowess. Fit the harder, less-yielding poly-bushes and you'll lose this.

Instrumentation and switchgear

Make a note of the car's instrumentation on the move. The speedometer can sometimes be noisy on the go, with audible clicks a feature, which means that the cable will need replacing or re-fitting and re-aligning at the speedo end to eliminate noise. Sometimes, at the gearbox end, the nylon worm drive wears or cracks in its housing, which also leads to an audible clicking. Although the part is out of production now, remanufactured parts made out of steel are available. Don't be too concerned if the fuel gauge dances about like a demented banshee. Again, they (really do) all do that! Ideally, you'll have familiarised yourself with the steering column stalks which control nearly everything, including the heater fan! Check that everything works as replacement of the column stalks is costly.

All Alfasuds and Sprints are fitted with a height adjustable steering wheel. Make sure this works.

Steering

All Alfasuds and Sprints are equipped with a height-adjustable steering column. Make sure this works. Check that the steering wheel is in its correct position with the road wheels in the straight ahead position. Wheel alignment is a pain to adjust on the Alfasud! If steering is stiff on the move, this indicates that the front strut top mounts and bearings need replacing. Any roughness or excess vibration felt through the steering wheel can be the result of worn-out driveshaft CV joints.

Further checks

After your test drive, before you switch off the engine, get out of the car and check for oil smoke, which is likely to be worn valve guides. Switching off the engine, run your finger around the inside of the exhaust tailpipe. Any heavy black and sooty deposits here can indicate an excessively rich petrol mixture, which may well have been caused by poorly-set carburettors that have been meddled with.

Evaluation procedure

Add up your total score. **144 = Excellent; possibly concours; 108 = Good; 72 = Average; 36 = Poor.** Cars scoring over 101 will be completely useable and require only regular maintenance and care to maintain condition. Cars scoring between 36 and 74 will require full restoration. Cars scoring between 75 and 100 will require very careful assessment of the necessary restoration/repairs costs in order to reach a realistic value.

10 Auctions
– sold! Another way to buy your dream

Auction pros & cons
Pros: Prices will usually be lower than those of dealers or private sellers, and you might grab a real bargain on the day. Auctioneers have usually established clear title with the seller. At the venue you can usually examine documentation relating to the vehicle.

Cons: You have to rely on a sketchy catalogue description of condition & history. The opportunity to inspect is limited, and you cannot drive the car. Auction cars are often a little below par and may require some work. It's easy to overbid. There will usually be a buyer's premium to pay in addition to the auction hammer price.

Which auction?
Established auctioneers advertise their events in car magazines and on their website. A catalogue, or a simple printed list of the lots, might only be available a day or two ahead, though often lots are listed and pictured on auctioneers' websites much earlier. Contact the auction house to ask if previous auction selling prices are available, as this is useful information (details of past sales are often available on websites).

Catalogue, entry fee and payment details
Purchase of the catalogue of the vehicles in the auction often acts as a ticket, allowing two people to attend the viewing days and the auction. Catalogue details tend to be relatively brief, but will include information such as 'one owner from new, low mileage, full service history,' etc. It will also usually show a guide price to give you some idea of what to expect to pay, and will tell you what is charged as a 'buyer's premium.' The catalogue will also contain details of acceptable forms of payment.

At the fall of the hammer an immediate deposit is usually required; the balance payable within 24 hours. If the plan is to pay by cash, there may be a cash limit. Some auctions will accept payment by debit card. Sometimes credit or charge cards are acceptable, but will often incur an extra charge. A bank draft or bank transfer will have to be arranged in advance with your own bank as well as with the auction house. No car will be released before **all** payments are cleared. If delays occur in payment transfers, storage costs can accrue.

Buyer's premium
A buyer's premium will be added to the hammer price: **don't** forget to include this in your calculations. It is not usual for there to be a further state tax or local tax on the purchase price, and/or on the buyer's premium.

Viewing
In some instances it's possible to view on the day, or days before, as well as in the hours prior to, the auction. Auction officials will be available to help out by opening engine and luggage compartments, and allow you to inspect the interior. While the officials may start the engine for you, a test drive is out of the question. Crawling under and around the car as much as you want is permitted, but you can't suggest

that the car you are interested in be jacked up, or attempt to do the job yourself. You can also ask to see any available documentation.

Bidding
Before you take part in the auction, **decide your maximum bid – and stick to it!**

It may take a while for the auctioneer to reach the lot you are interested in, so use that time to observe how other bidders behave. When it's the turn of your car, attract the auctioneer's attention and make an early bid. The auctioneer will then look to you for a reaction every time another bid is made: usually, the bids will be in fixed increments until bidding slows, when smaller increments will often be accepted before the hammer falls. If you want to withdraw from the bidding, make sure the auctioneer understands your intentions – a vigorous shake of the head when he or she looks to you for the next bid should do the trick!

Assuming that you are the successful bidder, the auctioneer will note your card or paddle number, and from that moment on you will be responsible for the vehicle.

If the car is unsold, either because it failed to reach the reserve or because there was little interest, it may be possible to negotiate with the owner, via the auctioneer, after the sale is over.

Successful bid
There are two more thing to consider. How to get the car home, and insurance. If you can't drive the car, your own or a hired trailer is one mode of transport; another is to have the vehicle shipped using the facilities of a local company. The auction house will also have details of companies specialising in the transfer of cars.

Insurance for immediate cover can usually be purchased on site, but it may be more cost-effective to make arrangements with your own insurance company in advance, and then call to confirm full details.

eBay and other online auctions
eBay and other online auctions could bag you a car at a bargain price, though you'd be foolhardy to bid without examining the car first – something most vendors encourage. A useful feature of eBay is that the geographical location of the car is shown, so you can narrow your choices to those within a realistic radius of home. Be prepared to be outbid in the last few moments of the auction. Remember, your bid is binding, and it will be very, very difficult to get restitution in the case of a crooked vendor fleecing you – *caveat emptor!*

Be aware that some cars offered for sale in online auctions are 'ghost' cars. **Don't** part with **any** cash without being sure that the vehicle does actually exist, and is as described (usually pre-bidding inspection is possible).

Auctioneers
Barrett-Jackson www.barrett-jackson.com/ Bonhams www.bonhams.com/ British Car Auctions BCA) www.bca-europe.com or www.british-car-auctions.co.uk/ Cheffins www.cheffins.co.uk/ Christies www.christies.com/ Coys www.coys.co.uk/ eBay www.eBay.com/ H&H www.classic-auctions.co.uk/ RM www.rmauctions. com/ Shannons www.shannons.com.au/ Silver www.silverauctions.com

11 Paperwork
– correct documentation is essential!

The paper trail
Classic, collector and prestige cars usually come with a large portfolio of paperwork, accumulated and passed on by a succession of proud owners. This documentation represents the real history of the car; from it can be deduced the level of care it has received, how much it's been used, which specialists have worked on it, and the dates of major repairs/restorations. All of this information will be priceless to you as the new owner, so be very wary of cars with little paperwork to support their claimed history.

Registration documents
All countries/states have some form of registration for private vehicle, be it the American 'pink slip' system or the British 'log book' system.

It is essential to check that the registration document is genuine; that it relates to the car in question, and that all the vehicle's details are correctly recorded, including chassis/VIN and engine numbers (if these are shown). If you are buying from the previous owner, his or her name and address will be recorded in the document: this will not be the case if you are buying from a dealer.

In the UK, the current (Euro-aligned) registration document is called the V5C, and it is printed in coloured sections of blue, green and pink. The blue section relates to the car's specification; the green section has details of the new owner, and the pink section is sent to the DVLA in the UK when the car is sold. A small section in yellow deals with selling the car within the motor trade.

In the UK, the DVLA will provide details of earlier keepers of the vehicle upon payment of a small fee, and much can be learned in this way.

If the car has a foreign registration there may be expensive and time-consuming formalities to complete. Do you really want the hassle?

Roadworthiness certificate
Most country/state administrations require that vehicles are regularly tested to prove they are safe to use on the public highway, and do not produce excessive emissions. In the UK, this test (the 'MoT') is carried out at approved testing stations, for a fee. In the USA, the requirement varies, though most states insist on an emissions test every two years as a minimum, while the police are charged with pulling over unsafe-looking vehicles.

In the UK, the test is required on an annual basis once a vehicle becomes three years old. Of particular relevance for older cars is that the certificate issued includes a mileage reading, recorded at the test date and, therefore, an independent record of that car's history. Ask the seller if previous certificates are available.

Without an MoT the vehicle should be trailered to its new home, unless you insist that a valid MoT is part of the deal. (Not such a bad idea, this, as at least you will know the car was roadworthy on the day it was tested.)

Road licence
Every country/state charges some kind of tax for the use of its road system, the actual form of the 'road licence' and how it is displayed varying enormously, country-to-country and state-to-state.

Whatever the form of the road licence, it must relate to the vehicle carrying it, and must be present and valid if the car is to be legally driven on the public highway. The value of the licence will depend on the length of time it will continue to be valid.

In the UK, if a car is untaxed because it has not been used for a period of time, the owner has to inform the licensing authorities by means of a 'SORN' (Statutory Off Road Notification), otherwise he or she will be liable for a fine. Moreover, the vehicle's date-related registration number will be lost, and there will be a painful amount of paperwork to get it re-registered.

Also in the UK, from 1 October 2014, it was no longer necessary to display a tax disc of a vehicle as evidence of having current and valid VED (Vehicle Excise Duty). This did not, sadly, mean the end of annual car tax, but it does have implications for buying and selling cars.

When buying a used car, any remaining tax can no longer be transferred to the buyer, who must tax the vehicle before using it. The vendor, in turn, automatically receives a refund for the remaining tax (provided they have notified the DVLA of the sale), although the refund will be for full calendar months only. This means that if a vehicle is sold one week into a new month, both vendor and buyer pays to tax the vehicle for the remainder of that month! Remember that if your car has been SORNed, it cannot legally be driven on UK roads. The car must be taxed before use. To find out if your car is taxed, log on to www.gov.uk/check-vehicle-tax.

Certificates of authenticity
For many makes of collectible cars, it is possible to obtain a certificate attesting to its age and authenticity (eg engine and chassis numbers, paint colour and trim). These are sometimes called 'Heritage Certificates,' and if the car comes with one of these, this is definitely a bonus. If you'd like one, the relevant owner's club is the best starting point.

If the car has been used in European classic car rallies it may have a FIVA (Federation Internationale des Vehicules Anciens) certificate. The so-called 'FIVA passport,' or 'FIVA Vehicle Identity Card,' enables organisers and participants to recognise whether or not a particular vehicle is suitable for individual events. If you want to obtain such a certificate go to www.fbhvc.co.uk or www.fiva.org. Similar organisations exist in other countries, too.

Valuation certificate
Hopefully, the vendor will have a recent valuation certificate, or letter signed by a recognised expert stating what they believe the particular car to be worth (such documents, together with photos, are usually required in order to secure 'agreed value' insurance). Generally, such documents should act only as confirmation of your own assessment of the car rather than a guarantee of value, as the expert has probably not seen the car in the flesh. The easiest way to find out how to obtain a formal valuation is to contact the owner's club.

Service history
Often, these cars will have been serviced at home by enthusiastic (and hopefully capable) owners for a good number of years. Nevertheless, try to obtain as much service history and other paperwork pertaining to the car as you can. Naturally, dealer stamps, or specialist garage receipts score most points in the value stakes. However, anything helps in the great authenticity game, with items such as original bill of sale,

If the engine has been rebuilt, ask for photographic evidence.

The quality of work should be evident from the photographs. New cambelts and tensioners have been fitted here: essential for engine life.

A new water pump has been fitted here: a very important service schedule item.

From the photographs, check for attention to detail.

handbook, parts invoices and repair bills all adding to the car's provenance. Even a brochure correct to the year of the car's manufacture is a useful and interesting document, which you could well have to search hard to find in future years. If the seller claims that the car has been restored, expect to see receipts and other such evidence from a specialist restorer.

If the seller claims to have carried out regular servicing, ask what work was completed and when, and seek evidence of it having been done. Your assessment of the car's overall condition should tell you whether the seller's claims are genuine.

Restoration photographs

If the seller tells you that the car has been restored, then expect to be shown a series of photographs taken while the restoration was under way. Pictures taken at various stages, and from various angles, should help gauge the thoroughness of the work. If you buy the car, ask if you can have the photographs, as they form an important part of the vehicle's history. It's surprising how many sellers are happy to part with their car and accept your cash, but want to hang on to their photographs! In the latter event, you may be able to persuade the vendor to give you a set of copies or let you get one made.

Bodywork restoration should be photographically documented.

If the vendor tells you that the car has had a bare metal respray, there should be a photo to verify this.

Check on the quality of this work.

At this stage, the car has received its primer coat ready for final prep.

The final top coat. It is absolutely essential that the primer has been allowed to dry fully before the final coat, as any moisture present here will cause problems down the line.

12 What's it worth?

– let your head rule your heart

Condition

If the car you've been looking at is really bad, then you've probably not bothered to use the marking system in Chapter 9: Serious evaluation, and may not even have got as far as using that chapter at all!

If you did use the marking system in Chapter 9, you'll know whether the car is in Excellent (maybe concours), Good, Average or Poor condition, or, perhaps, somewhere in-between these categories.

Many classic/collector car magazines run a regular price guide. If you haven't bought the latest issues, do so now, and compare their suggested values for the model you are thinking of buying. Also, look at the auction prices they're reporting. Values have been fairly stable for some time, but some models will always be more sought-after than others. Trends can change, too. Published values tend to vary from one magazine to another, as do their condition scales, so read the guidance notes they provide very carefully. Bear in mind that a car which truly is a recent show winner could be worth more than the highest scale published.

Assuming that the car you have in mind is not in show/concours state, relate the level of condition you judge the car to be in with the appropriate guide price. How does the figure compare with the asking price? Before you start haggling with the seller, consider what affect any variation from standard specification might have on the car's value.

If you are buying from a dealer, remember there will be a dealer's premium on the price.

Desirable options/extras

Not so much of an optional extra, but a very desirable feature of the Alfasud and Sprint range was the fact that, post-1980, all cars received much improved rust-proofing, applied by the factory, so any car manufactured after this date will be much more likely to have survived.

If you value your comfort, Alfasuds made after April 1980 had wider and plusher front seats. Similarly, cars produced after November 1981 had revised, taller transmission ratios, which gave more relaxed cruising in top gear, and an improvement in fuel economy, so are considered the most popular and user-friendly, being better suited to regular use.

Driver and passenger comfort, and levels of equipment improved with each Series of the Berlina and Sprint, although, for the ultimate in luxury, the Series III Gold Cloverleaf saloons, with their lavish upholstery, electric windows and manual tinted glass sunroof, are the ones to have. They had headlight washers, too, as standard.

The equivalent model in South Africa was known as the Alfa Romeo Superhatch 1.5, while, in Malaysia, all home-assembled 'suds had luxuries such as front seat lumbar support adjustment, and even air-conditioning throughout the range.

Special Edition models of the Sprint Coupés are becoming the most sought-after on the market, with the Plus, Trofeo, and Speciale versions attracting a 5-10 per cent premium over standard Sprints, partly due to their relative rarity. Similarly, the later Series III Sprint models with the full Zender bodykit fitted as standard equipment are worth slightly more than their unadorned brethren. Giardinettas (not specifically covered in this guide, but subject to similar inspection procedures) command slightly higher prices because there are just so few remaining worldwide.

The Alfasud Giardinetta. A rarity!

Undesirable features

There's something of an enigma here. Very early Series I saloons are considered by many to be the Alfasud in its purest form, free from the later Series' bodykits. They are, of course, the rarest, too, which also makes them the most sought-after. But therein lies the rub, as they were neither the best-built or best-equipped versions out there. Early Alfasuds ran into a series of reliability and quality problems, with trim literally falling off and chrome plating flaking almost as soon as the cars had left the factory. Some owners found that the external hinges of the boot lid broke off quite easily, too.

Dynamically, the earliest cars had their shortcomings. Flat spots on the carburettor could lead to potentially lethal outcomes. In a number of awkward or dangerous situations, such as when pulling out of a junction, some drivers found themselves without power, resulting in near-accidents. Certainly, the wide spacing of ratios in the original four-speed gearbox didn't help the situation particularly.

You may find, even when the steering geometry is spot-on, that the overall effort needed to steer an Alfasud or Sprint is too great, compared to what you're used to with a modern car. Some Alfasuds and Sprints have had power assisted steering retro-fitted by using all the (compatible) components from the later Alfa 33.

So, for the purist, there's a choice to make: desirability over drivability? It's up to you ...

Striking a deal

Negotiate on the basis of your condition assessment, the car's mileage, and fault rectification cost. Also take into account the car's specification. Be realistic about the value, but don't be completely intractable: a small compromise on the part of the vendor or buyer will often facilitate a deal at little real cost.

13 Do you really want to restore?
– it'll take longer and cost more than you think

Let's be clear, here. You may think you've found an Alfasud that requires just a little work, or alternatively, the car you're thinking of buying may well be in need of a full restoration. Well, to repeat the theme of this guide, keep your eyes wide open; ignore those rose-tinted specs, and keep it real because, frighteningly, whether you choose to carry out a full off-the-road renovation or to, perhaps, embark on a rolling restoration to return your car to its former glory, either way, the cost is likely to be entirely similar! Honestly. And this is especially true if you intend to pay someone to do the work for you.

Salvageable, but how would you like to tackle it?

By far the biggest cost involved in carrying out any restoration or remedial work is for labour, with an hourly rate that can, and does, vary enormously. There are many Alfa Romeo specialists out there who, to all intents and purposes, are undoubtedly enthusiastic and passionate about the marque, and who seem to want to work on cars for the sheer love of it. But, obviously, they do have a business to run and a living to make, so keep this in mind. Whatever (or whoever) you choose, it'll not be cheap.

If a professional restoration is the road you've chosen, this is where being a member of an owner's club will pay dividends, as such organisations will be able to put you in touch with a specialist in your area, whose many recommendations are the result of personal experience, vouching for the quality of work carried out.

Restorers generally work in one of two ways. They will either insist on inspecting and assessing the car to arrive at a quotation or estimate before any work is undertaken, or else they may prefer to start the restoration, keeping a log to invoice you for the total number of hours put in. So again, the news is that whatever or whoever you choose, it'll not be cheap. In any case, it's important that you make regular visits to the restorer to gauge progress, verify the quality of the work, and keep an eye on costs. It's a good idea to take photographs at various stages of the restoration, too: see examples in the previous chapter.

On the other hand, you may decide that you want to carry out the job yourself if you feel you have the necessary skills, facilities, inclination, and the all-important time. If this is the route you intend to take, then beware.

Do you have the facilities?

Classic car magazines and websites are full of cars for sale, described as 'unfinished projects,' where the owner has simply given up. There'll be a good reason for this: a loss of interest or patience, or money problems. Can you honestly see yourself taking on one of these unfinished projects, or starting a project yourself in the honest belief that you can complete the work needed?

If you're still attracted by this idea, to maintain interest and to trim costs, it may be better to tackle some of the work that you feel confident about yourself, and then involve a professional to carry out the more difficult aspects of the restoration. In some instances, too, your interest might well be maintained if you decide to source all the parts needed for the work yourself (the thrill of the chase!) from specialists at home or from literally all over the world via the internet – be they hard-to-find mechanical items or body panels – then employing a professional (if they are willing to do so) on a labour-only basis.

Whether you choose to do the work entirely yourself, have a professional take care of it, or take the 50-50 self/professional route, patience is key, as your car is likely to be off the road for some time, and will require taxing and testing again should either expire during the course of the restoration.

If you're taking on an abandoned project, check on the quality of the work done previously.

This Sprint needs just a little work to make it perfect: a rolling restoration, perhaps?

An alternative here is to buy a roadworthy car with a view to carrying out a rolling restoration. Keeping the car on the road while gradually restoring it might well help out in terms of retaining enthusiasm, and keeping control of costs.

Of course, if the car that you're buying is really poor then you may decide to take on a full 'nut-and-bolt' restoration, where its poor condition may not necessarily be an issue as long as it's structurally sound or structurally salvageable; remembering that some structural components are irreparable. If you do decide that this type of thorough restoration is the way to go, be prepared to wait a long time for the work to be completed, especially if you hand over the car to a professional restorer, who'll have many other projects on the go, as is the nature of his business.

So, all things considered, the question you need to ask yourself is this: do I really, truly, honestly want to take on a home or professional restoration, bearing in mind it's going to be easier (and definitely cheaper in the long run!) to buy a really good Alfasud or Sprint at a fair price in the first place?

It's your choice …

Best as a parts donor car, or as the basis for a full 'nut and bolt' type restoration?

14 Paint problems
– bad complexion, including dimples, pimples and bubbles

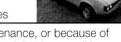

Paint faults generally occur due to lack of protection/maintenance, or because of poor preparation prior to a respray or touch-up. Some of the following conditions may be present in the car you're looking at –

Orange peel
This shows up as an uneven paint surface, similar in appearance to the skin of an orange. The fault is caused by the failure of atomized paint droplets to flow into each other when they hit the surface. It's sometimes possible to sand out the effect with proprietary paint cutting/rubbing compound, or very fine grades of abrasive paper. A respray may be necessary in severe cases. Consult a bodywork repairer/paint shop for advice on the particular car.

Cracking
Severe cases are likely to have been caused by too heavy an application of paint (or filler beneath the paint). Also, not stirring the paint sufficiently before application can lead to the components being improperly mixed, and cracking can result. Incompatibility with the paint already on the panel can have a similar effect. To rectify the problem, it is necessary to rub down to a smooth, sound finish before respraying the problem area.

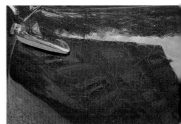

Crazing
Sometimes the paint takes on a crazed rather than a cracked appearance when the problems mentioned under 'Cracking' are present. This problem can also be caused by a reaction between the underlying surface and the paint. Paint removal and respraying the problem area is usually the only solution.

Blistering
This is almost always caused by corrosion of the metal beneath the paint. Usually, perforation will be found in the metal, and the damage will usually be worse than that suggested by the area of blistering. The metal will have to be repaired before repainting.

Micro-blistering
Usually the result of an economy respray where inadequate heating has allowed moisture to settle on the car before spraying. Consult a paint specialist,

but usually damaged paint will have to be removed before a partial or full respray. It can also be caused by car covers that don't 'breathe.'

Fading
Some colours, especially reds, are prone to fading if subjected to strong sunlight for long periods without the benefit of polish protection. Sometimes, proprietary paint restorers and/or paint cutting/rubbing compounds will retrieve the situation. Often a respray is the only real solution.

Peeling
Peeling is often a problem with metallic paintwork when the sealing lacquer becomes damaged and begins to peel off. Poorly applied paint may also peel. The remedy is to strip and start again!

Dimples
Dimples in the paintwork are caused by the residue of polish (particularly silicone types) not being removed properly before respraying. Paint removal and repainting is the only solution.

Dents
Small dents are usually easily cured by the 'Dentmaster' or equivalent process, which sucks or pushes out the dent (as long as the paint surface is still intact). Companies offering dent removal services usually come to your home: consult your telephone directory.

www.velocebooks.com / www.veloce.co.uk
Details of all current books • New book news • Special offers • Gift vouchers • Forum

49

15 Problems due to lack of use

– just like their owners, Alfasuds need exercise!

Cars, like people, are at their most efficient if they take regular exercise. A run of at least ten miles once a week is recommended for classics.

Seized components: brakes

On all but the last Series Sprint, the pistons in the rear brake callipers can seize. Underuse is the biggest cause of issues with the rear brakes. If the car has been standing for a while, glazing can also occur on the brake pad surfaces, reducing their effectiveness. Hard application of the brake pedal with the car reversing at moderate speed every so often will keep the rears in good order once the pistons/pads are freed off.

Late Series Sprints, with their braking system inherited from the Alfa Romeo 33, have rear drum brakes, the shoes of which can seize on or become glazed due to underuse. Slave cylinders within the rear drums can leak over time, and the handbrake (parking brake) cable can seize, too.

Handbrakes (parking brakes) on all other Alfasud or Sprint models operate on their front wheels by means of a lever incorporated into the front callipers. The lever can seize with underuse, and the cable and linkages can rust.

Seized components: clutch

The clutch may seize if the plate becomes stuck to the flywheel because of corrosion. The clutch actuation is hydraulic, so the slave cylinder, in particular, is prone to seizure or weeping of fluid over time. Remember that all Alfasuds and Sprints exhibit clutch chatter to some degree, so this, in itself, needn't necessarily indicate that there is a fault.

Seized components: timing belts and tensioners

There are two timing belts on the flat-four boxer engine: one for each bank of cylinders. The belts can perish over time, and the belt tensioners can seize, resulting in snapped belts and resultant engine damage. Ideally, for peace of mind, these components should be replaced on any new purchase. A timing belt kit will cost you far less than a full engine rebuild!

Fluids

Old, acidic oil can corrode bearings. Uninhibited coolant can corrode internal waterways. Lack of antifreeze can cause core plugs to be pushed out, and even cracks in the block or head. Silt settling and solidifying in both the engine block and the radiator can cause overheating.

Brake fluid absorbs water from the atmosphere, and should be renewed every two years. Old fluid with a high water content can cause corrosion and pistons/callipers to seize (freeze), and can cause brake failure when the water turns to vapour, near to hot braking components.

Tyre problems

Tyres that have borne the weight of the car in a single position for some time will develop flat spots, resulting in some (usually temporary) vibration. The tyre walls may have cracks or (blister-type) bulges, meaning that new tyres are needed.

Shock absorbers (dampers)
With lack of use, the dampers will lose their elasticity, or even seize. Creaking, groaning and stiff suspension are signs of this problem. Rubber suspension mountings and bushes can perish over time, and have a detrimental effect on the 'sud's sublime handling.

Rubber and plastic
Radiator hoses may have perished and split, possibly resulting in the loss of all coolant. Fan belts can perish, and water pump bearings can seize as a result of down-time. Window and door seals can harden and leak. Gaiters/boots can crack. Wiper blades will harden.

Electrics
The battery will be of little use if it has not been charged for many months. Earthing/grounding problems are common when the connections have corroded. Old bullet- and spade-type electrical connectors commonly rust/corrode, and will require disconnecting, cleaning and protection (eg Vaseline). Sparkplug electrodes will often have corroded in an unused engine. This is especially true if the car is fitted with its original Golden Lodge sparkplugs, which have four electrodes, but even more modern single electrode plugs can suffer this fault, too. Wiring insulation can harden and fail, and the multi-connectors in the loom can become corroded.

Rotting exhaust system
Exhaust gas contains a high water content, so exhaust systems corrode very quickly from the inside when the car is not used. Because of the engine's flat-four configuration, the front downpipes are a four-into-two-into one design, and are especially prone to corrosion damage due to the car standing for any length of time. These can be expensive to replace.

www.velocebooks.com / www.veloce.co.uk
Details of all current books • New book news • Special offers • Gift vouchers • Forum

51

16 The Community

Clubs

Alfa Romeo Owner's Club UK and Ireland
aroc-uk.com

AROC Alfasud Register UK
Colin Metcalfe, alfasud-register@aroc-uk.com

SCARB (NL)
alfaclub.nl/site/

Alfa Romeo Owner's Club (HK)
hkalfaclub.net

Alfa Romeo Klub Danmark (DK)
alfaklub.dk

Alfa Romeo Owner's Club of New Zealand (NZ)
arocnz.org.nz

Alfa Romeo Owner's Club of Australia
alfaclub.org.au

Der Alfaclub Deutschland eV (DE)
alfaclub.de

AROASA (SA)
alfaclub.co.za

Parts

Contact your club, or use the internet to find specialists in your country

Alfasud Parts Online
Peter Grummitt, alfasud-parts.co.uk

Just Suds
John Christopher, justsuds.co.uk

Mr Sud
Stephen Parry, mrsud.co.uk

Berterlsbeck
myalfa.eu

Alfa Panels
Bob Wright, highwoodalfa.com/bob2/index.html

Alfa Service
alfa-service.com

Torjay Tuning
torjay-tuning.hu

Alfa Restoration
alfa-restoration.co.uk/shop

Brinkmann
https://italiancarparts-shop.de

The Spare Place
thespareplace.com.au

The Italian Job
italianjobauto.com

Squadra Sportiva
shop.alfisti.net

Restoration/servicing

Contact your club or use the internet to find specialists in your country

MGS Coachworks
Mike Spenceley, mgscoachworks.com

CP Garage Services
Euan Colbron, cpgarageservicesdundee.co.uk

MDZ Italtec
mdzitaltec.co.uk

David Thomas Garages
davidthomasgarages.co.uk

Bianco Auto Developments
bianco-alfa.com

MWT Automotive Services
mwtautomotive.co.uk

Alfa Aid
alfaaid.co.uk

Gonnella Brothers
gonnellabrothers.co.uk

Sunnyside Garage
alfafiatservice.co.uk

Alfa Workshop
Jamie Porter
alfaworkshop.co.uk

Ferdi's Garage
ferdisgarage.co.uk

Advantage VRS Ltd
advantagedundee.co.uk

Alfashop
alfashop.co.uk

Broughty Ferry Auto Services
broughtyferryautoservices.co.uk

Other websites
Classic Alfa Forum
classicalfaforum.co.uk

Alfa Bulletin Board
alfabb.com

Alfasud Giardinetta page
alfasud-giardinetta.net

Tim's Alfasud Page
alfasud.alfisti.net

Books
The Alfasud. A Collector's Guide
David Owen
ISBN 978-0-947981-00-6

Alfa Romeo Spider, Alfasud and Alfetta GT. The Complete Story
David G Styles
ISBN 978-1-852236-36-6

Alfa Romeo Alfasud (Italian text)
Giancarlo Catarsi
ISBN 978-8-879114-92-9

How Your Car Works
Arvid Linde
ISBN 978-1-845843-90-8

The Essential Driver's Handbook
Bruce Grant-Braham
978-1-845845-32-2

www.velocebooks.com / www.veloce.co.uk
Details of all current books • New book news • Special offers • Gift vouchers • Forum

53

17 Vital statistics
– essential data at your fingertips

Specifications vary from country to country, so it's important that you know your market. Cars assembled at the Brits, South Africa plant differed from Italian-built ones in that, under a trade agreement in force at the time of their construction, after the base cars had been built up from the CKD kit, a large percentage of parts and components to finish the vehicles had to be locally made and sourced, to be fitted on the production line. As a consequence, you see slightly differing interior trim, steering wheels, dashboard and mirrors to European models.

The Alfasud Series III produced in Brits and was called the **Alfa Romeo Export**. The five-door saloon version of the Export got the name **Super Hatch 1.5** and was very similar to the European Alfasud 1.5 Quadrifoglio Oro (Gold Cloverleaf).

Top of
the range
Alfasud Gold
Cloverleaf.

The Sprint was also built in Brits. The Series III, known as the Sprint 1.5 Quadrifoglio Verde or Green Cloverleaf in Europe, was simply called Sprint Mk3 in South Africa. There were no further important differences compared to the European versions, although, interestingly, on the late model cars, Alfa Romeo SA never incorporated the Alfa 33's floorpan and brake system to the Sprint, and continued building it in Brits with inboard front and outboard rear disc brakes.

Alfa Romeo Italy also sent CKD kits to Malaysia, where they were completed. These cars were actually plusher than their European counterparts, and featured such luxuries as air-conditioning and lumbar support adjustment to the front seats. Another important difference over the European models was that, starting with the Series II Alfasuds, all Berlinas produced at the Kuala Lumpur plant received the ti's front four-headlight grille, dashboard (including the extra gauges), wheelarch extensions and rear spoiler. Cars assembled at Car Assembly Ltd at Marsa in Malta, however, were generally similar specification to European models. The market has recently seen a trend for these overseas-produced Alfasuds and Sprints, which are beginning to get more popular. As a consequence, these models command a 5% or so price premium over and above European examples. We've already seen the Alfasud and Sprint's UK timeline in Chapter 4, but now let's look at the cars' specifications and overall factory production figures in chronological order.

Alfasud Berlina (Saloon)

Series I: 1972-1977

Alfasud: four-door saloon: Type 901A: The very first incarnation of Alfa Romeo's revolutionary front-wheel drive small car with a boxer engine in very basic specification (rubber floor covering, minimum instrumentation, foot-operated manual screen wash) as launched at the Turin Motor Show in November 1971.
Engine: Type 30100: 1186cc: 63bhp: 4-speed transmission
Chassis numbers: AS*5000001*901A to AS*5022350*901A (1972)
Chassis numbers: AS*5022351*901A to AS*5099900*901A (1973)
Chassis numbers: AS*5099901*901A to AS*5168400*901A (1974)
Chassis numbers: AS*5168401*901A to AS*5176850*901A (1975)

Alfasud ti: two-door saloon: Type 901C: Sports version of the standard car. Rear and front chin spoilers. Sports interior and dashboard with engine power increase due to twin-choke single carburettor. 5-speed close-ratio gearbox improved acceleration.
Engine: Type 30104: 1186cc: 68bhp: 5-speed transmission
Chassis numbers: AS*5320011*901C to AS*5321450*901C (1973)
Chassis numbers: AS*5321451*901C to AS*5351442*901C (1974)
Chassis numbers: AS*5351443*901C to AS*5420287*901C (1975)
Chassis numbers: AS*5420288*901C to AS*5454448*901C (1976)

Alfasud: four-door saloon: Type 901D1: Brake servo now fitted as standard. Heated rear window, cigarette lighter, rev counter and front headrests all available as optional extras.
Engine: Type 30102: 1186cc: 63bhp: 4-speed transmission
Chassis numbers: AS*5000001*901D to AS*5000500*901D (1974)

Alfasud N & Alfasud L: four-door saloon: Type 901D: Alfasud base model (Type 901D1) re-designated Alfasud N. Wiper arms painted black. Received modified single-choke carburetion and driveshaft couplings were uprated to reduce vibration at the steering wheel.
  In addition, the Alfasud L, a more luxurious version of the N, received exterior embellishments; interior upgrades including carpets to replace the N's rubber mats and electronically-controlled windscreen washers. Rev counter still an optional extra.
Engine: Type 30102: 1186cc: 63bhp: 4-speed transmission
Chassis numbers: AS*5000001*901D to AS*5000500*901D (1974)
Chassis numbers: AS*5000501*901D to AS*5078500*901D (1975)

Alfasud 5M: four-door saloon: Type 901D: The Alfasud N and L models were discontinued to be gradually replaced by the 5M (5 Marce or 5-speed) model in single Luxury trim level.
Engine: Type 30102: 1186cc: 63bhp: 5-speed transmission
Chassis numbers: AS*5078501*901D to AS*5087103*901D (1976)
Chassis numbers: AS*5100001*901D to AS*5141747*901D (1976)
Chassis numbers: AS*5150001*901D to AS*5148899*901D (1976)
Chassis numbers: AS*5158900*901D to AS*5217459*901D (1977)

Alfasud ti 1.3: two-door saloon: Type 901G: Increased performance from larger 1286cc version of the boxer engine.
Engine: Type 30184: 1286cc: 76bhp: 5-speed transmission
Chassis numbers: AS*5000001*901C to AS*5006499*901C (1977)
Chassis numbers: AS*5006400*901C to AS*5030600*901C (1978)

Series II: 1977 -1979

Alfasud 1.2 Super: Type 901D: four-door saloon: Type 901D: The first of the second Series cars. Increased rust-proofing applied at the factory. Exterior modifications included large stainless steel bumpers with black polypropylene inserts front and rear and black radiator grille. Stainless steel also used to trim the door window frames while the bonnet (hood) air intakes and rear body pillars were also black. Interior was completely new with new seats and cloth inserts to the door cards and revised dashboard and instrumentation.
Engine: Type 30102: 1186cc: 63bhp: 5-speed transmission
Chassis numbers: AS*5158900*901D to AS*5217459*901D (1977)
Chassis numbers: AS*5270153*901D to AS*5295800*901D (1978)
Chassis numbers: AS*5295801*901D to AS*5232499*901D (1978)

Chassis numbers: ZAS901D00*0523500 to ZAS901D00*0531400 (1978)

Alfasud 1.3 Super: four-door saloon: Type 901F: Specification as 1.2 Super above but with larger 1286cc engine
Engine: Type 30180: 1286cc: 68bhp: 5-speed transmission
Chassis numbers: AS*5000001*901F to AS*5007200*901F (1977)
Chassis numbers: AS*5007201*901F to AS*5040000*901F (1978)

Alfasud 1.3 Super: four-door saloon: Type 901F2: The 1.3 Super was now offered with a slightly larger capacity engine of 1351cc from the recently introduced Sprint but with a lower compression ratio and a single-choke carburettor.
Engine: Type 30160: 1351cc: 71bhp: 5-speed transmission
Chassis numbers: AS*5020001*901F to AS*5040001*901F (1978)
Chassis numbers: AS*5040002*901F to AS*5065999*901F (1979)

Alfasud ti 1.3: two-door saloon: Type 901G2: The Series II version of the ti with a new 1351cc engine to replace the old 1286cc unit. Interior and exterior modifications as per the second series saloon but with the addition of a new design tail spoiler and black wheelarch extensions and sill covers.
Engine: Type 30164: 1351cc: 79bhp: 5-speed transmission
Chassis numbers: AS*5015000*901G to AS*5030600*901G (1978)
Chassis numbers: AS*5030601*901G to AS*504999*901G (1979)
Chassis numbers: ZAS901G20*05050000 to ZAS901G20*05051404 (1979)

Alfasud ti 1.5: two-door saloon: Type 901G1: Series improvements as the Alfasud ti 1.3 but fitted with a 1490cc boxer engine with a twin-choke carburettor.
Engine: Type 30124: 1490cc: 85bhp: 5-speed transmission
Chassis numbers: AS*5015000*901G to AS*5030600*901G (1978)
Chassis numbers: AS*5030601*901G to AS*5049999*901G (1979)
Chassis numbers: ZAS901G10*05050000 to ZAS901G10*05051404 (1979)

Alfasud 1.5 Super: four-door saloon: Type 901F1: A four-door version of the ti 1.5 in Super trim.
Engine: Type 30124: 1490cc: 85bhp: 5-speed transmission
Chassis numbers: AS*5020001*901F to AS*5040001*901F (1978)
Chassis numbers: AS*5040002*901F to AS*5065999*901F (1979)

Alfasud 1.3 Super: four-door saloon: Type 901F3: The 1.3 Super from model year 1979.
Performance: Engine Type 30164: 1351cc: 71bhp: 5-speed transmission.
Chassis numbers: ZAS901F30*05066000*901F to ZAS01F30*05071000 (1979)

Alfasud 1.5 Super: four-door saloon: Type 901F4: This version of the Super adopted the ti 1.5 boxer engine giving almost sports car-like performance.
Engine: Type 30124: 1490cc: 85bhp: 5-speed transmission
Chassis numbers: ZAS901F40*05066000 to ZAS 901F40*05071000 (1979)

Series III: 1979-1984

Alfasud ti 1.3: two-door saloon: Type 901G4: The uprated 1351cc engine from the Alfasud Sprint 1.3 now fitted to the ti 1.3 saloon with two twin-choke carburettors. Fittings were updated in common with the third Series.
Engine: Type 30168: 1351cc: 86bhp: 5-speed transmission
Chassis numbers: ZAS901G40*05051405 to ZAS901G40*05052300 (1979)

Alfasud ti 1.5: two-door saloon: Type 901G5: As the ti 1.3 above but the uprated engine from the Alfasud Sprint Veloce 1.5 was fitted to the ti 1.5 saloon with two twin-choke carburettors, together with higher compression ratio and revised profile camshafts. Fittings were updated in common with the third Series.
Engine: Type 30128: 1490cc: 95bhp: 5-speed transmission
Chassis numbers: ZAS901G50*05051405 to ZAS901G50*05052300 (1979)

Alfasud 1.2 Super: four-door saloon: Type 901D5: This version of the 1.2 Super was given a twin-choke carburettor. Fittings were updated in common with the third Series.
Engine: Type 30102: 1186cc: 63bhp: 4-speed transmission
Chassis numbers: ZAS901D50*05331401 to 05370500 (1980)

Alfasud 1.2 Super: four-door saloon: Type 901D4: As Type 901D5 above but with 5-speed transmission.
Engine: Type 30104: 1186cc: 63bhp: 5-speed transmission
Chassis numbers: ZAS901D50*05331401 to *05370500 (1980)

Alfasud 1.3 Super: four-door saloon: Type 901F3: Fitted with a single-choke carburettor. Fittings were updated in common with the third Series.
Engine: Type 30164: 1351cc: 71bhp: 5-speed transmission
Chassis numbers: ZAS901F30*05071001 to *05096046 (1980)

Alfasud 1.3 Super: four-door saloon: Type 901F3A: Fitted with a twin-choke carburettor. Fittings were updated in common with the third Series.
Engine: Type 30164: 1351cc: 79bhp: 5-speed transmission
Chassis numbers: ZAS901F30*05096047 to *05100999 (1980)

Alfasud 1.5: four-door saloon: Type 901F4: Fittings were updated in common with the third Series.
Engine: Type 30124: 1490cc: 85bhp: 5-speed transmission
Chassis numbers: ZAS901F40*05071001 to *05096046 (1980)
Chassis numbers: ZAS901F40*05096047 to *05100999 (1980)

Alfasud ti 1.3: two-door saloon: Type 901G4: All Series III 'suds received a styling upgrade. Externally, there were new bumper bars, new grilles, black door handles and stylised badges in relief to the rear pillars. Tail lights now extended into the boot lid and Giulietta style wheels were fitted as standard. Internally, there was a re-designed and more modern dashboard – bigger front seats and revised door panels. Ti models had black plastic wheelarch extensions, sill covers and tail spoiler.
Engine Type: 30168: 1351cc: 79bhp: 5-speed transmission
Chassis numbers: ZAS901G40*05052301 to *05063300 (1980)
Chassis numbers: ZAS901G40*05063301 to *05066000 (1981)

Alfasud ti 1.5: two-door saloon: Type 901G5: Third series upgrades as ti 1.3 above but fitted with larger 1490cc boxer engine.
Engine Type: 30128: 1490cc: 95bhp: 5-speed transmission
Chassis numbers: ZAS901G50*05052301 to *05063300 (1980)

Alfasud 1.2 Super: four-door saloon: Type 901D4A: 1981 model year.
Engine: Type 30104: 1186cc: 68bhp: 5-speed transmission (Normal Ratios)
Chassis numbers: ZAS901D40*05370501 to ZAS901D40*05419000 (1981)

Alfasud 1.2 Super: four-door saloon: Type 901D4C: 1981 model year as above but receiving revised long-ratio gearbox for more relaxed cruising.
Engine: Type 30104: 1186cc: 68bhp: 5-speed transmission (Long Ratios)
Chassis numbers: ZAS901D40*05419001 to ZAS901D40*05447750 (1981)

Alfasud 1.3 Super: three-door saloon: Type 901F3A: Now available as a hatchback. This version was fitted with 2 twin-choke carburettors.
Engine: Type 30164: 1351cc: 79bhp: 5-speed transmission (Normal Ratios)
Chassis numbers: ZAS901F30*05101000 to ZAS901F30*05127999 (1981)

Alfasud 1.3 Super: four-door saloon: Type 901F3B: As Type 901F3A above but four-door bodyshell with boot (trunk).
Engine: Type 30164: 1351cc: 79bhp: 5-speed transmission (Long Ratios)
Chassis numbers: ZAS901F30*05128000 to ZAS901F30*05135300 (1981)
Chassis numbers: ZAS901F30*05135300 to ZAS901F30*05136915 (1982)

Alfasud 1.5: three-door saloon: Type 901F4A: Now available as a hatchback with 1490cc boxer engine with a twin-choke carburettor.
Engine: Type 30124: 1490cc: 85bhp: 5-speed transmission (Normal Ratios)
Chassis numbers: ZAS901F40*05101000 to ZAS901F40*05127999 (1981)

Alfasud 1.5: three-door saloon: Type 901F4B: Hatchback as Type 901F4A above but receiving revised long-ratio gearbox for more relaxed cruising.
Engine: Type 30124: 1490cc: 85bhp: 5-speed transmission (Long Ratios)
Chassis numbers: ZAS901F40*05128000 to ZAS901F40*05135300 (1981)
Chassis numbers: ZAS901F40*05135301 to ZAS901F40*05136915 (1982)

Alfasud ti 1.3: three-door saloon: Type 901G4A: Now offered as a three-door Hatchback. Electronic ignition now fitted as standard.
Engine: Type 30168: 1351cc: 86bhp: 5-speed transmission (Normal Ratios)
Chassis numbers: ZAS901G40*0566001 to ZAS901G40*05076999 (1981)

Alfasud ti 1.5: three-door saloon: Type 901G4B: Hatchback as Type 901G4A above but receiving revised long-ratio gearbox for more relaxed cruising.
Engine: Type 30168: 1351cc: 86bhp: 5-speed transmission (Long Ratios)
Chassis numbers: ZAS901G40*05077000 to ZAS901G40*05080900 (1981)
Chassis numbers: ZAS901G40*05080901 to ZAS901G40*05091999 (1982)

Alfasud ti 1.5: three-door saloon: Type 901G5A: Now offered as a three-door Hatchback. Electronic ignition now fitted as standard.
Engine: Type 30128: 1490cc: 95bhp: 5-speed transmission (Normal Ratios)
Chassis numbers: ZAS901G50*0566001 to *05076999 (1982)

Alfasud ti 1.5: three-door saloon: Type 901G4B: Hatchback as Type 901G5A above but receiving revised long-ratio gearbox for more relaxed cruising.
Engine: Type 30128: 1490cc: 95bhp: 5-speed transmission (Long Ratios)
Chassis numbers: ZAS901G50*05077000 to *05080900 (1981)
Chassis numbers: ZAS901G50*05080901 to *05093999 (1982)

Alfasud 1.3 Super: three-door saloon: Type 901F3C: Offered as a three-door Hatchback alternative to the 1.3 Super four-door and receiving revised long-ratio gearbox for more relaxed cruising.

Engine: Type 30164: 1351cc: 79bhp: 5-speed transmission (Long Ratios)
Chassis numbers: ZAS901F30*05136913 to *05170000 (1982)
Chassis numbers: ZAS901F30*05170001 to *05172000 (1983)

Alfasud 1.2 S & 1.2SC: five-door saloon: Type 901D4D:
Four-door saloon versions were discontinued to be replaced by the five-door Hatchback bodyshell. The only difference between the S (Super) and SC (Super Comfort) models was the interior finish.
Engine: Type 30104: 1186cc: 68bhp: 5-speed transmission (Long Ratios)
Chassis numbers: ZAS901D40*05419001 to *05447750 (1982)
Chassis numbers: ZAS901D40*05447751 to *05454600 (1983)

Alfasud 1.3SC: five-door saloon: Type 901F3D: Five-door Hatchback offered in SC (Super Comfort) trim level and fitted with larger 1351cc boxer engine.
Engine: Type 30164: 1351cc: 79bhp: 5-speed transmission (Long Ratios)
Chassis numbers: ZAS901F30*05137865 to *05170000 (1982)
Chassis numbers: ZAS901F30*05170001 to *05172000 (1983)

Alfasud 1.5SC: five-door saloon: Type 901F4C: Five-door Hatchback offered in SC (Super Comfort) trim level and fitted with larger 1490cc boxer engine with a twin-choke carburettor.
Engine: Type 30124: 1490cc: 85bhp: 5-speed transmission (Long Ratios)
Chassis numbers: ZAS901F40*05136916 to ZAS901F40*05170000 (1982)

Alfasud 1.5 Quadrifoglio Oro: five-door saloon: Type 901F4D: The Top of the Range (Gold Clover Leaf) Alfasud saloon, equipped with headlight washers, rear window wiper, colour-coded radiator grille and bumper inserts, electric windows, plush cord cloth upholstery, a new steering wheel in imitation wood to match the armrest inserts and bright chrome trim rings to the road wheels.
Engine: Type 30128: 1490cc: 95bhp: 5-speed transmission (Long Ratios)
Chassis numbers: ZAS901F40*05137865 to ZAS901F40*05170000 (1982)
Chassis numbers: ZAS901F40*05137865 to ZAS901F40*05172000 (1983)

Alfasud 1.3SC: three-door saloon: Type 901F3C: Now the only three door three-door Hatchback offered in the SC (Super Comfort) trim level range and fitted with the 1351cc boxer engine.
Engine: Type 30164: 1351cc: 79bhp: 5-speed transmission (Long Ratios)
Chassis numbers: ZAS901F30*05136913 to ZAS901F30*05170000 (1982)
Chassis numbers: ZAS901F30*05170001 to ZAS901F30*05172000 (1983)

Alfasud ti 1.5 Quadrifoglio Verde: three-door saloon: Type 901G5C: The highest performing Alfasud saloon so far, the Green Clover Leaf received different camshafts to increase power and give stronger acceleration. There were black front chin and small tail spoilers along with the black plastic wheelarch extensions and sill covers. The stylised Alfa Romeo shiels in the front grille was painted red and there were exclusive eight hole light alloy wheels for this model available in either metric or imperial sizes (not interchangeable).
Engine: Type 30146: 1490cc: 105bhp: 5-speed transmission (Long Ratios)
Chassis numbers: ZAS901G50*05092000 to *05093999 (1982)
Chassis numbers: ZAS901G50*05094000 to ZAS901G50*05093999 (1983)

Alfasud Sprint (Coupé)
Series I: 1976-1983

Alfasud Sprint: three-door Coupé: Type 902A: Giorgetto Giugiaro-designed three-door Hatchback Coupé adopting the saloon mechanicals and running gear.
Engine: Type 30164: 1351cc: 79bhp: 5-speed transmission
Chassis numbers: AS*5000001*902A to 5006350*902A (1976)
Chassis numbers: AS*5006351*902A to 5017781*902A (1977)
Chassis numbers: AS*5017782*902A to 5024999*902A (1978)

Alfasud Sprint 1.3: three-door Coupé: Type 902A3: Minor changes to trim and switchgear
Engine: Type 30164: 1351cc: 79bhp: 5-speed transmission
Chassis numbers: AS*5025000*902A to 5039999*902A (1978)
Chassis numbers: AS*5040000*902A to 5045999*902A (1979)

Alfasud Sprint 1.5: three-door Coupé: Type 902A1:
Increased power output thanks to 1490cc boxer engine with a twin-choke carburettor
Engine: Type 30124: 1490cc: 85bhp: 5-speed transmission
Chassis numbers: AS*5025000*902A to 5039999*902A (1978)
Chassis numbers: AS*5040000*902A to 5045999*902A (1979)

Alfasud Sprint 1.3 Veloce: three-door Coupé: Type 902A4:
1351cc boxer engine now fitted with two twin-choke carburettors for increased performance.
Engine: Type 30168: 1351cc: 86bhp: 5-speed transmission (Normal ratios)
Chassis numbers: ZAS902A40*05406000 to ZAS902A40*05055600 (1979)
Chassis numbers: ZAS902A40*05055601 to ZAS902A40*05070000 (1980)
Chassis numbers: ZAS902A40*05070001 to ZAS902A40*05079999 (1981)

Alfasud Sprint 1.3 Veloce: three-door Coupé: Type 902A4A:
As Type 902A4 above but receiving the long-ratio gearbox for greater fuel economy and more relaxed cruising.
Engine: Type 30168: 1351cc: 86bhp: 5-speed transmission (Long ratios)
Chassis numbers: ZAS902A40*05080000 to ZAS902A40*05089999 (1981)
Chassis numbers: ZAS902A40*05090000 to ZAS902A40*05092200 (1982)

Alfasud Sprint 1.5 Veloce: three-door Coupé: Type 902A5:
1490cc boxer engine now fitted with two twin-choke carburettors for increased performance.
Engine: Type 30128: 1490cc: 95bhp: 5-speed transmission (Normal ratios)
Chassis numbers: ZAS902A50*05406000 to ZAS902A50*05055600 (1979)
Chassis numbers: ZAS902A50*05055601 to ZAS902A50*05070000 (1980)
Chassis numbers: ZAS902A50*05070001 to ZAS902A50*05079999 (1981)

Alfasud Sprint 1.5 Veloce: three-door Coupé: Type 902A5A:
As Type 902A5 above but receiving the long-ratio gearbox for greater fuel economy and more relaxed cruising.
Engine: Type 30128: 1490cc: 95bhp: 5-speed transmission
Chassis numbers: ZAS902A50*05080000 to ZAS902A50*05089999 (1981)
Chassis numbers: ZAS902A50*05090000 to ZAS902A50*05092200 (1982)
Chassis numbers: ZAS902A50*05055601 to ZAS902A50*05070000 (1983)

Alfasud Sprint Plus: three-door Coupé: Type 902A5: Factory official Special Edition finished in unique bronze metallic paintwork with colour-matched road wheel centres with Velvet interior and imitation wood steering wheel. Total production was 2,000 cars of which only 700 were sold in its native Italy.
Engine: Type 30128: 1490cc: 95bhp: 5-speed transmission
Chassis numbers: Included between ZAS902A50*05070001 & ZAS902A50*05079999 (1981)

Alfasud Sprint 1.5 Veloce Trofeo: three-door Coupé: Type 902A5A: Factory official Special Edition built to celebrate the fact that Alfasud Sprints were now competing in the prestigious Alfasud Trophy (Trofeo Alfasud) racing series. Body colour was metallic grey with a deeper colour grey stripe running along its flanks. The alloy wheel centres were painted to match the dark grey body stripe as were the car's B-posts. Tweed upholstery and imitation wood steering wheel.
Engine: Type 30128: 1490cc: 95bhp: 5-speed transmission (Long Ratios)
Chassis numbers: ZAS902A50*05090000 to ZAS902A50*05092200 (1982)

Series II: 1983-1984
Sprint 1.3: three-door Coupé: Type 902A4A: Major Facelift to include a new grille, headlamps, wing mirrors, window surrounds and C-pillar vent grilles. Bumpers went from chrome to plastic and large plastic protective mouldings were added to the body sides with coloured piping. New design rear lights and black number plate mounting panel. Inside there were new cloth seats and a new design steering wheel and dashboard. Steel wheels and grey piping to body side panels.
Engine: Type 30168: 1351cc: 86bhp: 5-speed transmission (Normal ratios)
Chassis numbers: ZAS902A40*054092201 to ZAS902A40*05114300 (1983)
Chassis numbers: ZAS902A40*05114301 to ZAS902A40*05120500 (1984)

Sprint 1.5: three-door Coupé: Type 902A5A: Second series upgrades as Alfasud Sprint 1.3 above but fitted with larger 1490cc boxer engine. Steel wheels and red piping to body side panels.
Engine: Type 30128: 1490cc: 95bhp: 5-speed transmission (Normal ratios)
Chassis numbers: ZAS902A50*05406000 to ZAS902A50*05055600 (1983)
Chassis numbers: ZAS902A50*05055601 to ZAS902A50*05070000 (1984)

Sprint Quadrifigolio Verde: three-door Coupé: Type 902A5B: Second series upgrades as Alfasud Sprint 1.3 above but fitted with 1490cc boxer engine from Alfasud ti 1.5 Green Cloverleaf. Alloy wheels and green piping to body side panels.
Engine: Type 30146: 1490cc: 105bhp: 5-speed transmission (Normal Ratios)

Sprint Quadrifigolio Verde: three-door Coupé: Type 902A5C:
Engine: Type 30146: 1490cc: 105bhp: 5-speed transmission (Long Ratios)
Chassis numbers: ZAS902A50*05090000 to ZAS902A50*05114300 (1983)
Chassis numbers: ZAS902A50*05114301 to ZAS902A50*05120500 (1984)

Series III: 1984-1989
All Sprints produced from the end of 1984 received the Alfa Romeo 33 platform complete with the braking system of outboard front discs and rear drums with the handbrake operating on the rear wheels. This was to replace the inboard front discs and outboard rear discs

(with the handbrake operating on the front wheels) that all Alfasuds and Sprints had been fitted with up until this stage. These cars from this point became known as the **Alfa Romeo Sprint Series III.**

Sprint 1.3: three-door Coupé: Type 902A4A: Now with Alfa Romeo 33 floorpan, running gear and braking system.
Engine: Type 30168: 1351cc: 86bhp: 5-speed transmission (Normal ratios)
Chassis numbers: ZAS902A40*05120501 to ZAS902A40*05124899 (1985)
Chassis numbers: ZAS902A40*05124900 to ZAS902A40*05128600 (1986)
Chassis numbers: ZAS902A40*05128601 to ZAS902A40*05132125 (1987)

Sprint 1.3: three-door Coupé: Type 902A4B: Sprint 1.3 fitted with long-ratio gearbox for more relaxed cruising and greater fuel economy. Body side protection mouldings omitted and new design wheels.
Engine: Type 30168: 1351cc: 86bhp: 5-speed transmission (Long ratios)
Chassis numbers: ZAS902A40*05132126 to ZAS902A40*05132700 (1987)
Chassis numbers: ZAS902A40*05132701 to ZAS902A40*05132890 (1988)

Sprint Quadrifigolio Verde: three-door Coupé: Type 902A5B: Now with Alfa Romeo 33 floorpan, running gear and braking system.
Engine: Type 30146: 1490cc: 105BHP: 5-speed transmission (Normal Ratios)

Sprint Quadrifigolio Verde: three-door Coupé: Type 902A5C: Now with Alfa Romeo 33 floorpan, running gear and braking system.
Engine: Type 30146: 1490cc: 105bhp: 5-speed transmission (Long Ratios)
Chassis numbers: ZAS902A50*05120501 to ZAS902A50*05124899 (1985)
Chassis numbers: ZAS902A50*05124900 to ZAS902A50*05128600 (1986)
Chassis numbers: ZAS902A50*05128601 to ZAS902A50*05132047 (1987)

Sprint Quadrifigolio Verde: three-door Coupé: Type 902A5D: With Alfa Romeo 33 floorpan and braking system. Featured new engine taken from the 33 1.5 and body side protection mouldings omitted. New design wheels and tail spoiler.
Engine: Type 30508: 1490cc: 105bhp: 5-speed transmission
Chassis numbers: ZAS902A50*05132048 to ZAS902A50*05132700 (1987)
Chassis numbers: ZAS902A50*05132701 to ZAS902A50*05132891 (1988)

Sprint 1.7 Quadrifigolio Verde: three-door Coupé: Type 902A6: With Alfa Romeo 33 floorpan and braking system. It featured a new engine taken from the 33 1.7QV. Body side protection mouldings omitted and new design wheels and tail spoiler. Tweed covered Recaro-type seats internally along with a leather-covered steering wheel.
Engine: Type 30550: 1712cc: 118bhp: 5-speed transmission
Chassis numbers: ZAS902A60*05131698 to ZAS902A60*05132700 (1987)
Chassis numbers: ZAS902A60*05132701 to ZAS902A60*05132892 (1988)

From April 1987: In the UK-only, the Sprint 1.5 Veloce Green Cloverleaf was offered alongside the production Sprint 1.3 and the standard 1.5QV (Quadrifoglio Verde) models. Externally, the 1.5

The last of the line. The Sprint 1.7 Quadrifoglio Verde.

Veloce Green Cloverleaf varied from the standard 1.5 QV by the addition of a paint colour-matched Zender bodykit, side protection panels and door mirrors. The Sprint 1.7 QV could also be ordered as a 1.7 Veloce Green Cloverleaf in the UK with the addition of the same bodykit and colour-matched body parts as the 1.5 Veloce Green Cloverleaf.

Total production number Alfasud: 715,170 vehicles; Total production number Alfasud Ti: 185,665 vehicles; Total production number Sprint: 116,552 vehicles; Total recorded production run: 1,017,387 units.

Note that the chassis and engine numbers quoted are from published factory records. There were often gaps in the number ranges; consequently there are some inconsistencies and omissions present.

Giardinetta
Although not specifically covered in this Guide, for record purposes, here are the statistics for the Alfasud Giardinetta:

First Series
Alfasud Giardinetta: Type 904A: three-door Station Wagon:
The Giardinetta had the same technical characteristics as the Alfasud N saloon model but with a better finish and equipment including a heated rear screen. Although the design of the SW was very proficient, with its low floor and large payload, unfortunately the car's sales success didn't match expectations.

Engine: Type 30102: 1186cc: 63bhp: 4-speed transmission
Chassis numbers: AS*5000001*904A to AS*5005450*904A (1975)
Chassis numbers: AS*5005451*904A to AS*5007000*904A (1976)
Chassis numbers: AS*5007001*904A to AS*5007077*904A (1977)

Alfasud Giardinetta: Type 904A1: three-door Station Wagon:
Modified with 5-speed gearbox to allow more relaxed cruising and give better fuel economy.
Engine: Type 30102: 1186cc: 63bhp: 5-speed transmission.
Chassis numbers: AS*5007501*904A to AS*5008581*904A (1977)

Second Series
Alfasud Giardinetta: Type 904B: three-door Station Wagon:
Receives the larger 1286cc boxer engine.
Engine: Type 30180: 1286cc: 68bhp: 5-speed transmission
Chassis numbers: AS*5001251*904B to AS*5001750*904B (1978)

Alfasud Giardinetta: Type 904B2: three-door Station Wagon:
Offered with the 1351cc engine from the 1.3 Super saloon
Engine: Type 30102: 1351cc: 71bhp: 4-speed transmission.
Chassis numbers: AS*5001251*904B to AS*5001750*904B (1978)

Note! Production of the Giardinetta Type 904B2, which in 1979 had been given a different numbering sequence beginning 904B20 *50030001, ended in January 1981. Unfortunately, no chassis numbers are available for the 1979, 1980 and 1981 model years.

www.velocebooks.com / www.veloce.co.uk
Details of all current books • New book news • Special offers • Gift vouchers • Forum

59

The Essential Buyer's Guide™ series ...

... don't buy a vehicle until you've read one of these!

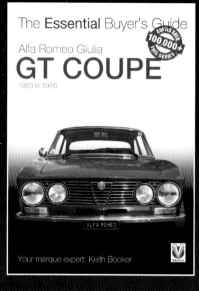
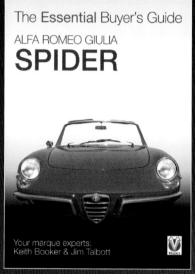